General Studies Series

TIMBER CONSTRUCTION FOR DEVELOPING COUNTRIES

Durability and Fire Resistance

UNITED NATIONS INDUSTRIAL DEVELOPMENT ORGANIZATION
Vienna, 1995

ID/SER.O/8

UNIDO PUBLICATION
UNIDO.92.8.E
ISBN 92-1-106282-9

The term "billion" signifies a thousand million.

References to tonnes are to metric tonnes.

The following technical abbreviations are used:

    BFCA   borofluoride-chrome-arsenic (preservative)
    CCA   copper-chrome-arsenic (preservative)

Abbreviation of organizations:

    CSIRO   Commonwealth Scientific and Industrial Research Organization

PREFACE

Whether grown in a particular country or not, wood is a virtually universal material that is familiar to people all over the world. It is used for many purposes but principally for construction, furniture, packaging and other specialized uses such as transmission poles, railway ties, matches and household articles. The United Nations Industrial Development Organization (UNIDO), which was established in 1967 to assist developing countries in their efforts to industrialize, has the responsibility within the United Nations system for assisting in the development of secondary woodworking industries and has carried out this responsibility since its inception at the national, regional and interregional levels by means of projects both large and small. UNIDO also assists by preparing manuals on topics that are common to the woodworking sectors of most countries.*

The lectures presented at the Timber Engineering Workshop (TEW), held from 2 to 20 May 1983 at Melbourne, Australia, are part of the continuing efforts of UNIDO to help engineers and specifiers appreciate the role that wood can play as a structural material. Collected in the form of 38 chapters, these lectures have been entitled <u>Timber Construction for Developing Countries</u>, which forms part of the General Studies Series. Two of the chapters make up this third volume of the collection, <u>Durability and Fire Resistance</u>. The TEW was organized by UNIDO with the cooperation of the Commonwealth Scientific and Industrial Research Organization (CSIRO) and was funded by a contribution made under the Australian Government's vote of aid to the United Nations Industrial Development Fund. Administrative support was provided by the Department of Industry and Commerce of the Australian Government. The remaining lectures (chapters), which cover a wide range of subjects, including case studies, are contained in four additional volumes, as shown in the table of contents.

Following the pattern established for other specialized technical training courses in this sector, notably the course on furniture and joinery and that on criteria for the selection of woodworking machinery,** the lectures were complemented by visits to sites and factories, discussion sessions and work assignments carried out by small groups of participants.

It is hoped that the publication of these lectures will lead to the greater use of timber as a structural material to help satisfy the tremendous need in the developing countries for domestic, agricultural, industrial and commercial buildings and for structures such as bridges. It is also hoped that the lectures will be of use to teachers in training institutes as well as to engineers and architects in public and private practice.

Readers should note that the examples cited often reflect Australian conditions and thus may not be wholly applicable to developing countries,

_____

*These activities are described more fully in the booklet <u>UNIDO for Industrialization: Wood Processing and Wood Products</u> (PI/78).

**The lectures for these two courses were collected and published as <u>Furniture and Joinery Industries for Developing Countries</u> (United Nations publication, Sales No. E.88.III.E.7) and <u>Technical Criteria for the Selection of Woodworking Machines</u> (UNIDO publication, Sales No. 92.1.E).

despite the widespread use of the Australian timber stress grading and strength grouping systems and despite the wide range of conditions encountered on the Australian subcontinent. Moreover, it must be remembered that some of the technology that is mentioned as having been new at the time of the Workshop (1983) may since then have been further developed. Similarly, standards and grading systems that were just being developed or introduced at that time have now become accepted. Readers should also note that the lectures were usually complemented by slides and other visual aids and by informal comments by the lecturer, which gave added depth of coverage.

CONTENTS*

---

*For the reader's convenience the contents of the four complementary volumes are also given here.

Introduction to Wood and Timber Engineering
(ID/SER.0/6)

I. Forest products resources
W. E. Hillis

II. Timber engineering and its applications in developing countries
John G. Stokes

III. Wood, the material
W. E. Hillis

IV. Mechanical properties of wood
Leslie D. Armstrong

V. Conversion of timber
Mervyn W. Page

IV. Seasoning of structural timber
F. J. Christensen

Structural Timber and Related Products
(ID/SER.0/7)

1. Characteristics of structural timber
Robert H. Leicester

II. Structural grading of timber
William G. Keating

III. Proof grading of timber
Robert H. Leicester

IV. Model of the timber grading process
Robert H. Leicester

V. Visual grading of timber
J. Hay

VI. Review of timber strength systems
William G. Keating

INTRODUCTION

Many developing countries are fortunate in having good resources of timber, but virtually all countries make considerable use of wood and wood products, whether home-grown or imported, for housing and other buildings, in both structural and non-structural applications, as well as for furniture and cabinet work and specialized uses. Although wood is a familiar material, it is all too often misunderstood or not fully appreciated since it exists in a great variety of types and qualities.

Some species, such as teak, oak and pine, are well known almost everywhere while others, such as beech, eucalyptus, acacia, mahogany and rosewood, are known primarily in particular regions. Still others, notably the merantis, lauans and keruing, which come from South-East Asia, have only recently been introduced to widespread use. Very many more species exist and are known locally and usually used to good purpose by those in the business. Also, plantations are now providing an increasing volume of wood.

The use of timber for construction is not new and, in fact, has a very long tradition. In many countries this tradition has unfortunately given way to the use of other materials - notably, concrete, steel and brick - whose large industries have successfully supported the development of design information and the teaching of methods for engineering them. This has not been so much the case for timber, despite considerable efforts by some research and development institutions in countries where timber and timber-framed construction have maintained a strong position. Usually the building methods are based on only a few well-known coniferous (softwood) species and a limited number of standard sizes and grades. For these, ample design aids exist, and relatively few problems are encountered by the very many builders involved.

Recent developments in computer-aided design and in factory-made components and fully prefabricated houses have led to better quality control and a decreased risk of site problems. Other modern timber engineering developments have enabled timber to be used with increasing confidence for an ever wider range of structures. This has been especially so in North America, Western Europe, Australia and New Zealand.

UNIDO feels that an important means of transferring this technology is the organization of specialized training courses that introduce engineers, architects and specifiers to the subject and draw their attention to the advantages of wood, as well as its disadvantages and potential problem areas, and also to reference sources. In this way, for particular projects or structures, wood will be fairly considered in competition with other materials and used when appropriate. Comparative costs, aesthetic considerations and tradition must naturally be taken into account in the context of each country and project, but it is hoped that the publication of these lectures will lead those involved to a rational approach to the use of wood in construction and remove some of the misunderstandings and misapprehensions all too often associated with this ancient yet modern material.

I. DURABILITY OF TIMBER

John Beesley*

Introduction

Wood preservation is the art of extending the useful life of timber in the service of mankind, with a time-scale measured in decades rather than in seasons or years. Although wood does not deteriorate just with the passing of time, some changes will take place in timber in service. Further, timber in service will be exposed to a variety of detrimental hazards that may operate continuously or intermittently, consecutively or concurrently. These forces may be consistent or they may change in both nature and severity during the service life of the timber.

By classifying these hazards and defining the various parameters that limit their effect or extension, it is possible to estimate the probable useful life of untreated timber and to assess the relative merits of substituting preservative-treated timber for untreated timber in new structures. In the case of existing buildings, this knowledge will be useful in assessing and anticipating the costs and consequences of taking no action, instituting remedial treatments, with minor repairs and replacements, or of undertaking a major reconstruction.

1. Mechanical deterioration

Timber that has split, shattered or broken, or that has been abraded and worn, is suffering from mechanical deterioration. If failure is due entirely to mechanical causes and has not been initiated or aggravated by other causes, the remedy is simple. The timber must be repaired or replaced with a harder, heavier, stronger piece of wood, or a facing must be employed to protect the piece from further wear. The possibility that poorly designed fastenings are inducing splitting should not be overlooked.

2. Chemical deterioration

Wood is relatively resistant to the action of most chemicals and, in fact, is frequently used in a wide range of industries in which chemical reactions are an integral part of the process. As a rule, wood is more resistant to the action of strong acids than strong alkalis. Chemical deterioration is uncommon in the structure of most buildings.

The first remedy, when chemical deterioration is suspected, is to examine the possibility of eliminating the source of the trouble. If that is not practical, it may be possible to protect the wood by some sort of barrier or coating.

3. Physical deterioration

Physical deterioration is best defined as deterioration due to the action of heat or moisture. Wood is a poor conductor of heat but can be ignited and

---

*Formerly an officer of CSIRO, Division of Chemical and Wood Technology, Melbourne, in conjunction with Chen Woo Chin, O. Collett, J. Creffield, C. D. Howick and D. McCarthy.

will burn when exposed to an ignition source. However, even when the wood is burning, the depth charred may not be very great during the early stages of combustion, and the loss of strength in a structural-sized member will be small. Prolonged exposure to high temperature, that is temperatures above the boiling point of water, will cause embrittlement and loss of strength, but such conditions are not common in dwellings. Under most normal conditions, it is possible to protect structural timbers from undue exposure to excessive heat either by removing or modifying the heat source or by inserting a suitable insulating material between the heat source and the timber.

Wood is hygroscopic and absorbs moisture from the atmosphere. Dry wood swells when wetted and wet wood shrinks when it dries. When, on the average, wood neither absorbs water from the atmosphere nor loses moisture to it, it is said to be in equilibrium with that particular atmosphere. For example, in Melbourne, the equilibrium moisture content for most timbers is about 14 per cent on an oven-dry weight basis in winter and about 11 per cent in summer, depending on the summer.

Shrinkage is not uniform either within a species or between species. In general, longitudinal shrinkage is least and tangential shrinkage is greatest, with radial shrinkage usually nearer the tangential than the longitudinal shrinkage. Hence there is a problem of differential movement where two components meet at right angles to one another as, for example, with the stile and the bottom rail of window joinery.

Most joinery and furniture is made from seasoned wood. If allowed to become wet, swelling will occur; this may cause joints to split. Glues are not always water-resistant, and any significant increase in moisture content is almost sure to adversely affect the surface finishes of paint, polish or varnish.

Prolonged exposure to very humid conditions could result in the growth of moulds and decay fungi.

4. Weathering

Wood that is freely exposed to the weather deteriorates. This deterioration is characterized by the silvering of the surface, which often also becomes eroded and irregular and may split. Weathering is a complex phenomenon attributed to a combination of the effects of exposure to ultraviolet light, heating and cooling, wetting and drying, erosion by wind-blown dust and other processes that in time lead to the bleaching and leaching of surface fibres and the development of surface checks. In some timbers, these surface checks are the foci of further weathering.

Paint, well-maintained, provides the best protection against weathering. Pigmented, water-repellent preservative stains are a cheaper and slightly less effective alternative. Unpigmented coatings (clear finishes) usually fail to filter out the ultraviolet light that causes bleaching and may fail to protect against the entry of water after a few months. That is to say, unpigmented coatings can be expected to break down, at the coating-timber interface, after a few months service.

5. Biological deterioration

The deterioration of timber attributed to living organisms is called biological deterioration. It is the form of unwanted deterioration most often encountered, and it is still insufficiently understood. In nature, biological agencies are responsible for recycling most living materials. It is only when man's needs conflict with what nature intended that problems arise.

Timber is an important building material. Before man learned to make use of it as a building material, trees grew in the forest, matured and died there. Throughout their life-cycle they were subjected to various forms of attack by insects and invasion and infection by fungi. Now, when timber may be required as a building material, it is still subject to the same hazards from insects and fungi. These invasions that occur during the growing period of the tree may affect the strength, quality or appearance of the timber obtained from the tree and may limit the uses to which it can be put.

Fortunately, much is known about the insects and fungi that affect the utilization of timber as a building material. This chapter describes the various forms of fungal deterioration that can occur in timber and describe the remedial measures, both natural and artifical, that may be taken to prevent, inhibit or reduce the extent of this deterioration. The success of such measures ultimately depends upon a thorough understanding of the conditions conducive to decay, the properties of the timbers themselves and the choice and availability of wood preservatives and preservative processes.

Measures that effectively control insect attack in building timbers in one country are likely to be equally effective in another country, provided the insect pest has been correctly identified and something is known about its habits. This information is also set out in this chapter, with particular reference to Australian conditions. For example, in Australia, the common powderpost borer, Lyctus brunneus Steph., is readily controlled by sodium fluoride or boron-based preservatives. These treatments will be just as efficacious elsewhere. What first needs to be done is to ascertain the lyctid-susceptibility of the local timbers and then to decide which of the several alterative treatments would be the most applicable under the prevailing circumstances.

A. The fungal deterioration of wood and its control

1. Natural durability and fungal attack

Timbers vary enormously in their natural resistance to insects and decay or other fungal attack. Some species, such as ironbark, teak and redwood (Sequoia spp.), are very resistant to both decay and insect attack and are known as durable species. Others, like radiata pine, coachwood and mountain ash, have very little natural resistance and are regarded as being non-durable, or even perishable. Also, since it is rare to find that the sapwood of a timber has any appreciable resistance to fungal attack, it must for all practical purposes be regarded as perishable unless it is properly treated with a wood preservative. Therefore, the natural durability of a timber species is always assessed by referring to the resistance of its mature heartwood to insect and fungal attack.

Because timbers vary so widely in the natural durability of their heartwood, it is necessary to have some form of classification for natural durability. The system most widely used throughout Australia was developed by CSIRO and has been adopted by the Standards Association of Australia. It recognizes four durability classes:

(a) Durability class 1. Species of the highest natural durability, e.g. grey box and yellow box, grey ironbark and red ironbark, wandoo and cypress pine;

(b) Durability class 2. Durable species, but not as good as class 1 species, e.g. red gum, jarrah, yellow stringybark and western red cedar;

(c) Durability class 3. Moderately durable species, e.g. southern blue gum, messmate, stringybark and karri;

(d) Durability class 4. Non-durable species or species of low natural resistance to fungal attack, e.g. mountain ash, manna gum, coachwood and sassafras, radiata pine and meranti.

This classification system is limited to the relative durability values of different timbers. It would be misleading to quantify the expected service life because of the infinite variety of conditions to which wood can be exposed in service. Under severe conditions, the service life achieved by the most durable species may not be much longer than that achieved by a species of moderate natural durability under conditions where the hazard is both mild and intermittent. However, under the same conditions of exposure, the higher the natural durability of a species the longer is its service life likely to be.

Unless otherwise stated, this system of classification refers to both decay resistance and resistance to attack by subterranean termites. Generally, resistance to decay, which is the most damaging form of fungal attack, parallels resistance to termite attack, but some Australian species, such as brush box, exhibit much higher resistance to termite attack than to decay. It should be noted, too, that where a parcel of timber contains mixed species, or the species is unknown, it is usually safest to regard the timbers as being of durability class 4. Also, some timbers, such as Douglas fir, that are rated at durability class 4 perform remarkably well when exposed to the weather if they have no ground contact. It should be recognized, therefore, that the CSIRO system of durability classification refers to ground contact conditions where decay and subterranean termite attack form a combined hazard.

The decay resistance of a timber is due mainly to the deposition of complex substances, the heartwood extractives, in the newly formed heartwood. Many of these are more or less toxic to fungi and insects and act as natural preservatives. Amongst the eucalypts, these substances appear to be polyphenolic compounds, which are related to the tannins. The precise chemical nature of many of these compounds has not yet been determined.

The decay resistance of timbers varies widely, not only between different species and between different trees of the same species but also within individual trees. The within-tree variation is mainly in the radial direction, with the outer (most newly formed) heartwood being the most durable part of the tree and the core or pith being relatively non-durable. The relatively low durability of the core is believed to be due in part to the lower resistance of the heartwood of a young tree and in part to the aging of the toxic extractives in the standing tree. This core, or brittle heart, which exists in most eucalypts, tends to become larger as the tree grows older, and it affects the recovery of useful timber from the log.

2. Facts about fungi

Fungi are plants, but not green plants. They lack chlorophyll, the substance that gives green plants their colour and enables them, in the presence of light, to synthesize sugars and starch from the carbon dioxide of the air and water from the soil. Since fungi do not have the capacity to synthesize their own nourishment from air and water, they get their nourishment by digesting organic matter, living as parasites (on living matter) or as saprophytes (on dead organic matter). The fungi that cause decay in timber live on the dead wood cells of the plant.

The fungal plant body consists of microscopic, branching, thread-like tubes called hyphae, which ramify through the nutrient source. Sometimes these hyphae spread over the surface of the host material to form a dense mat, which may be characteristic of the particular decay fungus present. This mat may also give rise to the fruiting body, the means by which these fungi sexually reproduce. With other fungi, including many wood-destroying fungi, the fruiting body may be fleshy, leathery or corky. Whether the fruiting body is a massive bracket or mushroom or a microscopic one borne on the mycelial mat, it is capable of releasing myriads of microscopic spores, each of which can develop into a new plant.

In broad terms, fungal attack on wood can take the form of surface mould, which can develop within two or three days. It is more likely to affect sapwood than heartwood but does not penetrate the timber. It may take the form of staining or discoloration that can penetrate deeply into sapwood within a few hours of the felling of a tree. The staining or discoloration may affect the heartwood, but it seldom has much effect on the strength properties of the sapwood although it may seriously mar its appearance. When fungal attack on wood takes the form of decay, or rot, there is a significant loss of strength. Some rots develop in the standing tree, while others affect timber in service.

In broad terms, all fungi that attack wood have the same basic requirements, whether they are moulds, stains or rots (fungi that produce decay, or loss of strength, in wood). Staining fungi can infect the living tree as well as freshly felled timber. Both moulds and stains can develop on susceptible timber in a very short time, while decay develops rather more slowly. If conditions favourable to fungal development are allowed to persist for an extended period of time, the timber can be expected to decay. The presence of surface moulds or staining is indicative of conditions that are, or have been, conducive to the development of decay. However, under suitable conditions, decay can develop without any evidence of moulding or staining.

3. Conditions necessary for fungal development

In general, five conditions must be satisfied before fungal development can occur, and the absence of any one of these may be sufficient to prevent it. Severe staining and moulding can develop in three or four days under favourable conditions, but for severe decay to develop, suitable conditions must persist for several weeks or longer.

A source of infection

Moulds, stains and decay-producing fungi spread by releasing millions of microscopic spores (fungal "seeds") into the air. Fungal spores contaminate most of the air and nearly all unprotected surfaces. Even in almost completely enclosed cavities in a structure, there will be some air exchange and, sooner or later, fungal spores will enter.

The spores of moulds and decay-producing fungi are so widespread that susceptible materials are almost certain to be affected whenever conditions suitable for fungal development occur. Further, once wood has started to decay, the rotted wood absorbs moisture more readily and retains it longer than does similar undecayed wood.

A supply of nutrients

Unlike green plants, which contain chlorophyll to enable them to synthesize sugars and starch from air and water in the presence of light, fungi lack chlorophyll and require an organic substrate upon which they grow through the action of enzymes such as cellulases, amylase, hemicellulase and ligninase. Moulds and stains derive their nourishment from the cell contents and not the cell walls, so they have little effect on strength properties. Rots, or decays, on the other hand, nourish themselves by dissolving the components of the cell wall, so they have a marked effect on mechanical properties. Their development can be accelerated by the presence of additional nutrients, especially nitrogenous fertilizers. Hence, decay can be very rapid in livestock transports, fertilizer plants and in timbers in contact with fertilized soil.

A supply of air

Since oxygen diffuses only very slowly through water, wood that is completely submerged in water or in waterlogged soil, such as foundation piles driven to the water table, decays at an extremely slow rate and needs no other protection against decay. Also, logs or chips stored under water in log ponds or under continuous water sprays remain sound for long periods. The moisture content of many types of freshly felled wood is so high, especially in the sapwood, that fungal attack is confined to the surface by the lack of oxygen further in, partly because the oxygen has been consumed by surface-growing fungi. The wood must therefore dry out to some extent before any appreciable decay or fungal staining can develop.

It might be thought that wood could be preserved by enclosing it completely in paint, fibreglass or plastic to exclude oxygen, but many of these materials are relatively pervious to oxygen. Since it is also very difficult to ensure that not even a pinprick can develop to admit oxygen or water, this method cannot be relied on.

Suitable temperature

Atmospheric temperatures are rarely major factors in decay since fungi can operate over a wide range of ambient temperatures. The optimum temperature for decay fungi is usually between 20° C and 30° C, so that decay is much more rapid in warmer localities, but most can still function down to 5° C and can cause slow decay even in cool stores. Most fungi can tolerate short exposures to even the highest atmospheric temperatures but are killed fairly rapidly if exposed to temperatures of 40°-50° C. Thus it is possible to arrest decay by heating wooden articles, for instance in a kiln, long enough for the innermost parts of the wood to come to these temperatures. This kills the fungi present but does not protect the wood from further infection.

A supply of moisture

All fungi need a supply of moisture. Without it, they die. It is well known that permanently dry wood never rots and, in fact, almost all fungi need both some free water in the cell cavity and the "bound" water in the cell wall. Decay normally occurs only at moisture contents above the fibre saturation point, which is between 30 and 35 per cent for most timbers. There may be slow decay by some fungi, especially soft rot fungi, at lower moisture contents, so it is usually considered that any wood with a moisture content of over 25 per cent is liable to decay.

The fungus itself can produce a considerable amount of water from the chemical decomposition of the wood, and this may help to keep the moisture content of the wood at a level favourable to fungus development.

The distribution of moisture within a piece of wood in service, or in storage, is usually very uneven. A moisture content of less than 25 per cent near the surface, or even a mean moisture content of less than 25 per cent, may still leave parts of the wood moist enough for decay. Moreover, most decay-producing fungi will remain alive, though inactive, for months in air-dry wood and will continue to grow sporadically in wood that is intermittently wet.

It is important to realize that by far the most effective means of protecting wood from fungal attack is to keep it dry. The great bulk of the timber used in buildings is never exposed to a decay hazard because it is too dry, and almost all the decay occuring in timber not in ground contact can be traced to wetting of the timber in ways that could have been easily and inexpensively avoided by thoughtful design and careful construction and maintenance.

4. Mould growth

Mould does not penetrate the timber but forms a powdery or cottony growth on the surface, where the fungi have grown on the food reserves that the tree has stored in the ray cells. Like blue stain, mould tends to be most severe on sapwood, and especially on sapwood with a high starch content. Its development depends not only on the moisture content of the wood but also on atmospheric humidity. Hence, it is most prevalent in warm, humid climates, on block-stacked timber or on moist timber held in a closed space, such as in a ship's hold. Mould does not penetrate through the cell walls and so has no effect on the strength of the wood. Since it is readily removed by brushing or, alternatively, by dressing the timber, its effect on appearance is not as serious as that of staining fungi.

Mould growth often occurs in combination with fungal stain, and its presence indicates that the wood is being, or has been, kept under undesirably moist conditions. It may interfere with the drying and gluing of timber and especially of veneers. Where control is desirable, it may usually be achieved with the same type of solution that is used for sap stain, perhaps at a higher concentration, e.g. 1 per cent sodium pentachlorophenate plus 1 per cent borax.

5. Fungal staining

Fungal staining is a common cause of degradation in timber. Discoloration, which is usually grey or blue grey, and sometimes brown, yellow or orange, occurs as wide longitudinal bands, usually confined to the sapwood of the timber. It is associated with the presence of hyphae within the wood. The colour is due to the colour of the hyphae, to the excretion of coloured material from them or to the production of abnormal colourations by the living cells of the tree under the stimulus of fungal attack. Although these fungi ramify through susceptible wood, as do decay fungi, they do not dissolve the wood substance but live mainly on the cell contents, especially starch. Like decay fungi, staining fungi are unable to develop in dry wood and possibly are inhibited by the lack of oxygen in water-soaked wood.

Staining is not accompanied by any pronounced loss of strength. Degradation consists almost entirely of the less attractive appearance of the wood. The discoloration caused by blue stain fungi is extremely difficult to remove by bleaching, and it becomes even more conspicuous when the timber is given a clear finish.   Some staining fungi can cause an appreciable loss in impact resistance, so wood required to have high impact strength should be free from blue stain.   Moreover, since the conditions required by the staining fungi are very similar to those favouring decay fungi, staining is a sign that incipient decay may also be present and be causing loss of strength.   Stained wood may be much more absorbent than sound wood, and this may be detrimental in wood preservation and perhaps in gluing.   Staining fungi may also affect the paint-holding qualities of the wood.

Infection of a log by staining fungi usually starts at cut ends, at areas where bark has been removed and at insect boreholes, especially those of pin-hole borers and of bark beetles.   It also starts in sawn boards immediately after sawing.   Infection is rapid under warm conditions, and surface treatments applied more than 48 hours, or even 24 hours, after felling or after sawing may be too late.

Sawn boards are protected by being dipped immediately after sawing in an anti-sap stain dip, which usually contains 0.5 per cent of sodium pentachlor-ophenate and 1.5 per cent of borax.   Recently, the fungicide Difolatan has become popular.   Dipping can be done either by hand or by passing the board on moving chains through a dipping trough.   This should give sufficient protec-tion to allow the boards to be air-seasoned without degradation.   The protec-tion of logs is more difficult, so it is important to extract and convert the logs as soon as possible after felling.   A stronger anti-stain solution, such as 2 per cent pentachlorophenol in light oil, together with an insecticide if borers are present, may be effective if it is applied to cut ends and barked areas within a few hours of felling.   Another good method is to store the logs under water sprays pending conversion [1].

6. Decay

The term decay is used to describe any type of fungal attack that, if allowed to continue unchecked, eventually causes severe loss of strength in the infected wood.   The fungi that cause decay grow through moist wood as a branching network of microscopic tubes, known as hyphae, that somewhat resem-bles the root system of a plant.   Within decaying wood, the individual hyphae are too small to be seen without the aid of a microscope; with a microscope, they are readily identifiable.   As the decay progresses, the hyphae often form wefts or fans of white cottony or fine silky material on the surface of the wood that is typical of the particular fungus species.   The fruit body is the organ of the fungus that produces millions of microscopic spores and releases them into the atmosphere to be disseminated by air currents, propagating the species.

Chemically, wood consists of a mixture of celluloses, hemicelluloses and lignin, all of which are insoluble.   When attacked by the fungi that cause decay, each hyphal tip within the wood secretes enzymes that dissolve the wood substance to form simpler, soluble products that can be absorbed and utilized by the fungus.   Brown rot fungi attack the cellulose and hemicellulose of the cell wall but are unable to destroy the lignin, which forms a major part of the wall substances.   This imparts a dark brown colour to the wood.   Since most of the strength of wood rests in the cellulose fibrils, a brown rot fungus will still destroy the wood.   In fact, by the time the wood has lost about one half its original weight through decay by a brown rot fungus, it can usually be reduced to a fine powder by rubbing between the fingers.   White rot fungi are able to attack the lignin as well as the celluloses and hemicellu-loses.   The removal of the lignin accounts for the bleached appearance of the decayed wood.   Some white rot fungi are able to destroy wood almost completely, reducing its original weight by about 98 per cent. The mechanical strength of wood may be seriously reduced by incipient decay, with little visible sign of fungal attack. Resistance to impact is likely to be affected first, so that timber required to have a high impact strength should be either pre-tested or carefully inspected for incipient decay. Decayed wood also absorbs water far more readily than similar sound wood. This fact should not be overlooked when timber is subjected to intermittent wetting, for once decay has started, the wood will take up more water with each wetting.

7. Types of decay: detection and appearance

Decay, especially beneath paint, is often detected only at a relatively late stage, usually as a result of the pronounced shrinkage or mechanical breaking of the affected wood. Where the wood surface is exposed, decay may often be detected from a localized darkening in colour, or from the development of checks in the wood on drying. Where a timber structure is being system- atically examined for the occurrence or distribution of decay, the most effective procedure is to drive a blunt instrument, such as a thin-bladed screwdriver, into the wood, when the decayed portion is readily detected by the lower resistance to penetration.

Decay may occur in the interior of a piece of wood, leaving an intact shell. Such internal decay may sometimes be detected by sounding, but the best method is to drill the wood (using, for example, a 6 mm bit in a small electric drill) and detect the decayed wood by its much lower resistance to drilling. Most decay causes the wood to break with a short brash or carrot-y fracture and may be tested for, especially in its early stages, by levering up splinters with a knife blade.

Four terms are used to describe some important types of decay.

Brown cubical rot

In brown cubical rot the wood becomes dark and soft and breaks with a definite brash or carrot-y fracture; on drying, it shrinks abnormally and checks both along and across the grain to form cubical pieces, which can even- tually be powdered in the hands. Brown cubical rot is caused by members of a class of higher fungi known as basidiomycetes, such as Serpula (Merulius), Coniophora and some species of Poria. It is a common form of decay in flooring, weatherboards and poles and also occurs in heart rots.

White stringy rot

In white stringy rot, the wood may not change much in colour at first, but it becomes yellowish or whitish in the later stages of decay. It becomes soft but does not shrink greatly in drying, and the highly decayed wood can be reduced to short stringy particles rather than to powder. It is caused by basidiomycetes such as Fuscoporia, Fomes and Trametes and is found in window joinery, weatherboards, house stumps (foundation piles) and heart rots, par- ticularly in hardwoods.

White pocket rot

In white pocket rot, the wood shows small, distinct whitish pockets sepa- rated by narrow bands of sound wood and does not change greatly upon drying. It is caused by basidiomycetes such as Fomes and Hymenochaete and is usually a heart rot, though it may also occur as a rot in poles or other large timbers.

Soft rot

In soft rot, the wood is usually darkened and shows a brash fracture, but it may be quite hard and show little change upon drying out. Surface soft rot usually dries out to show cubical checking like brown cubical rot but on a much smaller scale, with "cubes" 0.8 to 3 mm across. It is caused by fungi such as Chaetomium, Acremoniella and Doratomyces. Surface soft rot is common in cooling towers, on badly weathered fence rails etc., and on durable timbers in ground contact. It is much more severe in hardwoods than in softwoods.

These are the most readily recognized forms of decay, but there are other intermediate or less definite forms, which are described by other terms.

Dry rot

In Europe the term dry rot is used specifically to describe the decay caused by the fungus Serpula (Merulius) lacrymans, which is now also found in Australia. The term is misleading since it implies the rotting of dry timber, which is not possible. In Australia, the term dry rot is commonly used to describe decay that has occurred without an obvious source of moisture, usually as a result of condensation.

Wet rot

The term wet rot, which should also be avoided, is sometimes used for rot in very wet situations to distinguish it from dry rot. It usually refers to decay by Coniophora spp.

Heart rot

This refers to decay occurring in the standing tree, usually as a narrow central column. Heart rots may be brown cubical rots, white pocket rots or white stringy rots. While they reduce the strength of the material, and the reduction may extend well beyond the visible margin of the rot, they do not necessarily indicate that further trouble will occur in service. Most sawn timber is used in conditions that are too dry to allow decay, and even where moisture is present and the conditions appear suitable, many heart rot fungi do not appear to be able to continue their attack in sawn timber. Wood showing heart rots usually absorbs water much more readily than sound wood, and this may increase the decay hazard in some conditions.

8. Occurrence and control of decay

Decay of timbers in ground contact

All timber in contact with moist soil is at great risk of decay. Decay usually commences at or slightly below ground level, but it may occur at any depth up to 2 metres or even more, especially in sandy soils. When inspecting for decay, it is therefore desirable to excavate and probe well below ground level, and it may also be desirable to drill the timber since in many cases a shell of sound timber surrounds rotted wood.

The most effective means of preventing decay in timbers in ground contact is the use of highly durable or preservative-impregnated timber. However, even with preservative salt retentions in excess of 20 kg/m^3, soft rot can attack sapwood under certain conditions. The coating of new timber with creosote etc. has only a very short-term protective effect. Where decay is occurring in existing posts or stumps and replacement is difficult, it may be useful to apply a water-soluble diffusing preservative. This can be applied around the post as a bandage below soil level with an organic or inorganic diffusing preservative on the inside and an impervious plastic film on the outside to prevent diffusion into the soil. Such bandages are now commercially available for _in situ_ treatment.

Decay in building timbers above ground

Significant losses are caused each year by decay in above-ground timbers, and this has led to a reluctance to use wood for some applications. Such decay can almost always be avoided by correct building practice, but considerable use of remedial measures is required in existing buildings. The decay usually occurs either in external joinery, fascias and weatherboards or in flooring.

External woodwork

External woodwork is subject to intermittent wetting, and decay is likely to occur when wetting is frequent or of long duration, when the timber is relatively absorbent or when the wood is unable to dry out rapidly after wetting. All three factors are important. It is very important to reduce the frequency and duration of the periods in which water is in contact with the wood. This cannot be done by normal painting alone, since movement at the joints will crack the paint film and allow water to seep in. With weatherboards, important means are the provision of adequate roof overhang, the repair of leaking or blocked guttering, and the positioning of shrubs and creepers away from the wall so that surface water dries off rapidly. Since water absorption is particularly rapid in the end grain, the use of cover strips over the ends of the weatherboards, or of end priming, is particularly effective. With window joinery, the design should be such that water drains off completely and does not collect in tiny pools. The top faces of all sills, horizontal sashes, rails etc. should be sloped, and all joints should be inspected to ensure that water drains away from them. Excessive condensation on the inner side of the windows in, for example, sun rooms and bathrooms, means that water can collect on the inner sills and sashes and lead to decay. Adequate ventilation can often prevent this.

The reduction of water absorption during the wetting period is also important. The use of highly absorbent timbers such as ramin, sassafras or pine sapwood can lead to very rapid decay in painted window joinery, its development being assisted by the fact that once decay has commenced the wood becomes even more absorbent. A most effective means of reducing water absorption is the use of water-repellent preservatives. A number of these light organic solvent preservatives are now on the market. They greatly improve the performance of external joinery and weatherboards, not only by reducing the likelihood of decay but also by reducing paint failure near the ends of the boards. They are also effective in preserving the appearance of unpainted external woodwork in natural finish construction. Although best applied by dipping the completely prefabricated assembly, they are also valuable for the _in situ_ treatment of cut ends etc. and even for the remedial treatment of the joints in existing woodwork. For this last application, the preservative is brushed on liberally and allowed to seep into the joints when the woodwork is in a very dry condition.

Finally, there must be a means of drying out the timber after wetting. This is often completely neglected. It is difficult to prevent water uptake completely, so if water is absorbed, for example, by a piece of wood painted on all sides except the end through which the water is coming, drying out is extremely slow and the wood may remain wet enough for long enough to allow decay. If one face is unpainted, drying out will be much more rapid. Priming of the back face of weatherboards, though it may improve dimensional stability, slows down drying, enables water to penetrate further from the wetted ends and so favours decay. Placing impervious sarking or reflective insulation directly under weatherboards also greatly reduces drying and is an important factor contributing to decay. In many types of external joinery, such as window walls, it may be desirable to leave one face of each member - the underside of a horizontal rail - unpainted, or painted lightly with a "breathing" paint to reduce the chance of decay.

Flooring

Some floorings may be exposed to abnormal decay hazards as a result of wetting. This occurs on verandas or open porches exposed to rain and in bathrooms or laundry rooms subjected to plumbing leaks and condensation.

Porch floors should be of highly durable timber spaced slightly apart to prevent the accumulation of water or dirt between the boards. Water-repellent preservatives should be used to protect the end grain. Bathroom floors should be of durable or preservative-treated timber with provision for good ventilation.

The main cause of decay in flooring is the condensation of water vapour from the sub-floor space, and it is important to realize just how this process occurs. Even if dry on top, the soil below a building is always moist at lower levels and there is a continuous release of water vapour into the sub-floor space. If the flooring above this is at a much lower temperature than the soil, as it usually is in winter, some of the water vapour will condense on the flooring and may wet it sufficiently to allow decay. If there is adequate ventilation of the sub-floor space, the water vapour may be swept out before condensation takes place, and condensate formed in exceptionally cold, still weather can readily dry out. Similarly, if the floor is bare or covered only with carpet, water vapour can readily escape through the floor to the drier room air, but if the floor is covered with vinyl tiles, rubber (which includes underlays) linoleum or other impervious materials, such escape is impossible.

The usual method of preventing floor decay, therefore, is the provision of adequate sub-floor ventilation. Although this varies a great deal with climate and other factors, as an example it is suggested that in Victoria the ventilation system should provide vents with a minimum free air space of 110 cm^2 for every 1.5 m run of external wall and at least that amount in every internal sub-floor wall. (Most 23 x 15 cm pressed metal wall vents now sold have around 40 per cent free air space and are much more effective than some of the older-type terracotta "air bricks", which had less than about 6 per cent free air space.) This requirement may need to be exceeded where the minimum distance between opposite walls is over 10 m. It is also important that the movement of air through the ventilators should not be obstructed by joists or mortar drippings, or by shrubs, garden plantings or soil.

The provision of adequate ventilation is usually easy in residences but may be difficult in shops, where the sides may have party walls with adjoining buildings and where the floor is at pavement level. In these cases, normal cross-ventilation is impossible and floor vents appear to have little value. The use of vertical flues 15-20 cm in diameter from below the floor to above roof level at the "closed" end of the building, with liberal provision for air intake through sub-floor ventilators or floor vents at the opposite end, appears to be a promising method. Blowing warm air into the sub-floor space, e.g. from store heating systems, is often suggested, but this method has many drawbacks. Apart from the cost of continuous operation and maintenance for many years, the system would have to be carefully designed to ensure that the warm air did not absorb moisture from one part of the space and deposit it in some colder area further on. In new buildings where concrete terraces or bathroom floors on solid fill would block normal ventilation, it may be desirable to lay 10-15 cm diameter ventilating pipes through the obstruction.

In all cases where it is difficult to provide sub-floor ventilation, full use should be made of the North American system of soil cover. This involves laying a sheet of polyethylene film, bituminous felt or other impervious and durable material over the soil below the floor, so that the movement of the water vapour from the soil to the sub-floor space is greatly reduced or practically eliminated. Such soil cover can be easily and cheaply installed in new construction. In existing buildings, it is often possible to roll the sheet out, even under a low floor. There is no need to completely seal the joints or edges in the cover and it is often of value if only a part of the soil is covered. The reduced amounts of water vapour coming through can then be coped with by a more modest ventilation system.

Wooden floors on concrete slabs may also be at risk of decay. Even if the concrete has been waterproofed, water vapour will move up through it, and even if the concrete contains or overlies an impervious plastic film, moisture can often seep in the edges, and the slab itself will release water vapour for many months. Such floors should always be ventilated, and it may be necessary to cover the concrete with plastic film, bitumen or vapour-impermeable paint between joists or nailing strips. (Any nailing strips set in the concrete should be of preservative-treated wood.)

These requirements for ventilation or soil cover where wooden floors are used over either soil or concrete should be carefully followed. Although the use of treated flooring will eliminate the risk of decay, some measures may still be necessary to reduce undesirable cupping or movement of the floor boards.

Miscellaneous building timbers

Decay can, of course, occur in parts of buildings other than external woodwork and flooring. Decay in beams and joists may occur because of condensation, as described for flooring. More usually it is caused by the seepage of water from masonry due to the failure or omission of a damp-proof course, or by the penetration of rain through solid masonry walls in old buildings. In new structures, this can be prevented by waterproofing the walls, by installing complete and permanent damp-proof courses, and by isolating timber from masonry by plastic sheet, galvanized iron or bitumen. In existing buildings, it may be possible to restrict the ingress of water by waterproofing or to insert a moisture barrier between timber and masonry. Helping the joists to dry out by improving the ventilation or by removing paint from them may be helpful. Where decay is sufficiently advanced to cause risk of failure, strengthening with treated timber or metal plates may be preferable to removal.

Decay in cold stores is often a serious problem and is usually due to water vapour coming from warm, moist outside air and condensing within the insulated walls. It can often be prevented by placing a vapour barrier on the outside of the wall. A vapour barrier should never be placed on the inside face of the wall. This would prevent the evaporation of water vapour into the drier air of the cold room, which usually has a low absolute water vapour content even if the relative humidity is high.

Decay in wood used as decking under flat membrane roofs may be caused either by leakage or by condensation within the roof structure, especially where the use of the room involves humid conditions. Because repairs in such a position would be very expensive, it is desirable to use treated timber, although a vapour barrier between the room and the decking, plus ventilation within the roof, may give adequate protection.

Decay in boats

Decay in wooden boats has become an increasingly serious problem in recent years. There has been a spectacular increase in the use of power boats for pleasure, and many of these are now used on inland rivers, lakes and reservoirs rather than in salt water. This tends to increase decay hazards partly because sea water acts as a mild preservative and inhibits many fungi, and partly because inland waters, being small and land-locked, are prone to still, damp days, which make it difficult to ventilate the boats and dry them out.

Decay may occur in any part of the craft: in the outer planking or plywood skin, in major structural members such as ribs or stern posts and in cabin linings. It is caused by dampness due to rainwater seepage, condensation, shipping of (fresh) water or seepage from the bilges.

Preventive measures include the use of preservative-impregnated timber and plywood wherever possible, especially for structural members where replacement costs would be high; the liberal use of water-repellent light organic solvent preservatives, especially on the end grain of wood and the edges of plywood; the adequate ventilation of all cavities within the boat; and the designing of decks, wheel-houses etc. so that rainwater drains off completely and cannot seep into joints. It is important to help wood to dry out by refraining from painting any interior timber unless it is essential to do so. Timber or plywood coated on all exposed faces with red lead or marine varnish can scarcely be expected to dry out.

An important control measure is the regular and systematic inspection of all parts of the boat for the first signs of decay, using a thin-bladed screwdriver as a probe. If decay is detected early, it can usually be remedied without much trouble. Remedial measures include replacing decayed wood; preventing rainwater seepage; improving ventilation; removing paint, linings etc. to provide better drying conditions; and in fresh water, using diffusing preservatives, e.g. borax, in the bilges.

Decay in cooling towers

Industrial development and the progress of air conditioning is leading to a great increase in the use of cooling towers, but many wooden cooling towers have been severely affected by decay, and there is a tendency to use other methods of cooling. Decay is usually in the form of surface soft rot, especially in the filling slats but also in other parts of the tower. However, brown rots can still occur. Pre-treatment of the timber with a highly fixed copper-chrome-arsenic preservative is the method now preferred for prolonging the life of cooling tower timbers in Australia. Where soft rot has occurrred in large existing towers, there are commercially available in situ treatments that deposit insoluble salts in the wood and appear to give a considerable increase in service life.

B. Wood-destroying insects: wood borers

1. General characteristics

Since under certain conditions various timbers may be attacked by wood borers of different types, it is important to be aware of the existence and habits of these pests. With some species of wood borer, an infestation can result in serious damage necessitating treatment and repair or replacement. With other species, little weakening is likely to occur and, unless a good appearance must be maintained, remedial action is unnecessary.

Most wood borers are beetles that at some stage of their development bore into wood for food or shelter. Beetles undergo complete metamorphosis, passing through four distinct stages of development: egg, larva, pupa and adult. The larvae of most wood borers actively tunnel in wood and derive their nourishment from it. With some exceptions, the only damage they cause as adult beetles is the flight hole made through the surface of the infested timber as they emerge. After emergence and mating, the female may lay eggs in the timber from which she emerged. Usually, the adults live for only a few weeks.

Some borers lay their eggs beneath the surface of the wood, others lay them in cracks and crevices or where one piece of timber abuts another. Some borers introduce the spores of a wood-rotting or wood-softening fungus with their eggs, others do not. Some species attack only green timber, although they can often complete their life cycle and emerge after the timber has dried out. Other species attack only seasoned timber. A knowledge of these characteristics and habits can assist in identifying the type of borer responsible for the damage. Appropriate action can then be taken.

Significant differences in a number of common borers and in their habits are shown in table 1. For simplicity, a division has been made between those species attacking standing trees and green timber and those that attack dry wood. Information is also given on methods of control, including a discussion of quarantine requirements in Australia.

2. Borers attacking standing trees and green timber

Pinhole borers

Pinhole borers are forest insects belonging to the families Platypodidai, Scolytidae or Lymexylonidae. They are capable of attacking both standing trees and freshly felled logs, but they do not and cannot initiate attack in dry timber. Attack may occur in a tree that has suffered external damage, but it is more likely to occur in felled logs, often shortly after felling. Most pinhole attacks occur in hardwoods, but softwoods are not immune from attack.

The members of the families Platypodidae and Scolytidae are often known as ambrosia beetles. Their attack is initiated by adult beetles boring into the timber, excavating tunnels and placing eggs within the timber at the termination of the various branches of the tunnels. These pinhole borers may thus be regarded as a distinct group among the wood-boring beetles, as it is the adult beetle, and not the larva, or grub, that causes damage to infested timber. After hatching from the eggs, larvae live and grow in the galleries constructed by the parent until they reach maturity, in from one to four months. They feed not on the wood but on a fungal or mould growth, termed "ambrosia", that is introduced into the galleries by the parents prior to egg-laying. Because this ambrosia requires moisture for its development, it will die out as the timber dries, and consequently the larvae will not survive. This is

Table 1. Characteristics of the more common borers a/

	Borers attacking standing trees and green timber				Borers attacking dry wood						
	Pinhole	Longicorn	Bostrychid	Siricid	Lyctus brunneus	Anobium punctatum	Calymmederus incisis	Ernobius nollis	Hylotrupes bajulus	Arbeodontus tristis	Anobium australiens
Timber Type	In Victoria mainly hardwoods	In Victoria mainly hardwoods	In Victoria mainly hardwoods	Softwoods, mainly pine	Hardwoods	Mainly softwoods	Softwoods. Queensland especially hoop pine	In Softwoods with bark	Mainly softwoods	N.Z. rimu, some pines	Softwoods and hardwoods usually with decay
Zone	Sapwood and heartwood	Sapwood and heartwood	Sapwood only	Mainly sapwood	Sapwood only	Mainly sapwood	Sapwood and heartwood	Mainly bark, some sapwood	Mainly sapwood	Sapwood and heartwood	Sapwood and heartwood
Larval Galleries Direction in timber	Straight across grain	Meandering along grain	Meandering along grain	Curved, random	Meandering along grain	Meandering, honeycombed	Meandering, honeycombed	Cambial zone only	Meandering, random	Meandering, random	Meandering, mainly along grain
Discoloration	Present	Absent	Absent	Absent	Absent	Absent	Absent	Absent	Absent	Absent	Absent
Frass (borer dust) Quantity	Slight	Slight	Copious	Tightly packed	Copious	Copious	Copious	Moderate	Copious	Moderate	Moderate
Description	Strands or powdery	Coarse and stringy	Fine and powdery	Coarse	Fine and powdery	Granular like salt	Granular	Granular and speckled	Granular to powdery	Coarse and compacted	Powdery, compacted
Flight holes Shape	Round	Oval	Round	Round	Round	Round	Round	Oval	Oval	Oval	Round
Diameter, mm	2 or less	6-10 (long axis)	1-6	3-6	1-2	2	2	2	Up to 6 (long axis)	About 6 (long axis)	2-5

a/ It is important to distinguish between the coniferous timbers, or softwoods, such as the pines, firs and spruces, and the hardwoods such as the eucalypts and the lightweight or "softer", hardwoods of the rain forests.

why pinhole borers attack only green timber and will not infest or re-infest once the wood has dried. With these species, the frass, or borer dust, takes the form of a loose powder that is ejected on the surface of the log, where it may lie in piles before falling off.

The larvae of the third family, Lymexylonidae, do not appear to depend on fungal material for nourishment, although their galleries are often discoloured. These larvae actively bore into the timber, ejecting compacted strands of frass. Lymexylids are not commonly found in the eastern states but are of considerable importance in Western Australia.

The galleries made in timber by species of Platypodidae and some species of Scolytidae are discoloured by the growth of the ambrosia fungus, and this dark staining may extend along the grain in the vicinity of the gallery or hole. For this reason, pinhole attack can affect the market value of timber. If the original attack occurred in the standing tree through a surface scar or wound, it will probably cease as the wound heals over, but when the apparently clean log is peeled for veneers, the stained punctures will be revealed. Some loss of quality must be expected in all timber infested by pinhole borers. However, where the timber is to be used as ordinary building scantling, pinhole attack is unlikely to cause significant degradation or loss of strength and may be equated with a similar number of small nail holes. In a load of scantling timber, very heavily infested pieces may have to be culled, but the remainder will be quite satisfactory for ordinary building purposes. A piece of scantling timber attacked by pinhole borers will not constitute a hazard to other timbers in the structure as these will be at least partially dry and therefore immune from pinhole borer attack.

Longicorn borers

The Cerambycidae is a family of beetles widely distributed throughout the world and popularly known as the longicorns or longhorns because of the length of their antennae (feelers). Although certain species of longicorn occur in sufficient numbers in various parts of the world to be of economic importance, they are essentially a forest pest, since most species can initiate attack only on living trees and green timber. Because of this, they can affect the amount of merchantable timber obtained from the tree, but they do not greatly detract from the performance of building timbers.

The actual wood boring is done during the larval period, which is usually from one to three years in the living tree. Adult beetles occasionally emerge from structural timbers or furniture. This may be explained by the fact that although most longicorns attack only green timber, they are able to complete their development in dry wood. In seasoned timber, where moisture contents are necessarily lower and the amount of starch present may be much less than in green wood, the larvae obtain less nourishment and thus their life cycle may be extended greatly. Periods in excess of 20 years have been recorded. However, if timber that has been attacked when green is subsequently kiln-dried, no larvae will emerge from it, as the temperatures normally used in kiln-drying schedules are sufficiently high to kill all stages. Most adult longicorns are medium to large beetles (20-50 mm in length) and are characterized by their antennae, which are generally as long as or longer than their bodies.

Although many hundreds of species regularly breed in Australia, only a limited number of species occur in sufficient quantities to be of any importance to timber users. In Australia the majority of longicorn attacks occur in green hardwoods, although in other countries some species readily infest softwoods. Attack is not necessarily confined to sapwood, as larvae may tunnel deep into the heartwood as they prepare to pupate.

The structural weakening of framing timbers by longicorn borers is unlikely. Most longicorns do not excavate timber extensively and although the galleries are large, they do not honeycomb the wood. As it is unusual to find more than one or two larvae in a piece of framing-sized timber, emergence is unlikely to be more than sparse. Except for a very few species, longicorns cannot re-infest the dry timber from which they have emerged, so further damage is improbable. In emerging from studs or other framing timbers, longicorns may cut through lining materials such as plaster or fibre walls. This does not mean that they are attacking the wall, but merely that the lining was impeding their egress. The flight hole disfigures the timber, but it can be filled and the surface finish restored. Emergence holes are usually isolated and scattered, are oval and 6-10 mm in diameter, and the margins are unstained. The galleries are usually across the grain, and the frass is often coarse and stringy.

Bostrychid borers

Auger beetles that belong to the family Bostrychidae do not initiate attack in living trees but can and do attack freshly felled logs and green timber. Timber is frequently attacked by bostrychids during seasoning but usually not after the wood approaches the fibre saturation point, i.e. about 30 per cent moisture content. These borers do not attack dry timber, so it is unusual for more than one generation to breed in any one piece of commercial timber. Like the longicorn borers, bostrychids can complete their life-cycles in, and subsequently emerge from, dry wood. Only the sapwood of hardwoods is susceptible to bostrychid attack. The eggs are laid by the female beetle at the ends of short tunnels bored into susceptible sapwood, and after hatching, the larvae tunnel in the sapwood, obtaining nourishment from the starch in the timber and subsequently emerging as adult beetles. The frass produced by the larvae is coarse-grained and often lumpy.

There are a large number of species of bostrychids. The adults are from 3 to 20 mm long. Apart from one species, <u>Bostrychopsis jesuita</u>, which is up to 20 mm in length, most common bostrychids such as <u>Mesoxylion collaris</u> are small beetles up to 6 mm long. The round emergence hole made by these more common species is usually about 2 mm in diameter, but flight holes made by other bostrychids vary from 1 to 6 mm in diameter according to the species. It is not unusual to find <u>M. collaris</u> emerging from scantlings during the first summer after a house has been constructed. In ordinary scantling timber they do not constitute a serious hazard, as they can infest only sapwood and cannot re-infest dry timber. However, they cause considerable degradation to decorative timber, and their presence is nearly always indicative of timber susceptible to attack by Lyctidae (the powder post beetle), which attacks timber of a similar type but at a lower moisture content.

Sirex wood wasp

Sirex is not a beetle but a wood wasp belonging to the family Siricidae. Originally a European timber pest, it has been introduced into many other countries.

Sirex attack is limited to softwoods, predominantly pine. All the trees attacked by siricid wasps in Europe are conifers and include the pines, the firs and spruces. In North America there are several species of siricid, each attacking a range of pines and some attacking firs, including Oregon (Douglas fir). Since siricid wood wasps attack only living trees, freshly felled logs and green timber, they are essentially a forest pest that kills trees there. As with other green timber pests, it is impossible for siricids to complete their life-cycle in dry timber and subsequently emerge. Experience has indicated that the most serious attack occurs on suppressed, damaged or burnt trees, but once infestation has become well established, the population build-up may lead to attack on apparently healthy trees.

Although sirex is a wasp, its life-cycle resembles that of the wood-boring beetles. The female wasp lays her eggs in the tree by inserting her ovipositor, or egg-laying apparatus, which operates like a thin tubular drill, through the bark and into the wood. At the same time, she introduces the spores of a wood-rotting fungus, probably to soften the wood around the egg. It is believed that these fungal spores are always injected whenever the ovipositor is inserted into the tree, and it is this fungus that kills the tree after it is taken up into the sap. After about two weeks, the eggs hatch into larvae, which initially feed near the surface and then bore into the tree towards the heart. The tunnels may be as much as 450 mm long and increase in thickness as the larvae grow. Larvel galleries are circular and meandering and usually tightly packed with rather coarse frass. Towards the end of the larval period, the larvae return to a point near the surface and, after pupation, the adult wasp chews its way out of the timber, leaving a round emergence hole up to 6 mm in diameter. It is interesting to record that Siricid females are capable of parthenogenesis. In other words, females can lay unfertilized eggs that subsequently hatch out, although always into males. The eggs of a fertilized female, however, will usually produce about equal numbers of males and females.

Although limited degradation is caused by siricid attack, the insect can be responsible for enormous economic loss by killing living trees. In Australia, strict quarantine control is exercised on the movement of timber from areas where Siricids are known to be active. The restrictions require that if any pine timber leaves the area to be milled, it must be either fumigated under quarantine supervision or kiln-dried. The only exception to this rule is timber to be milled to a thickness of 6 mm or less, as it is unlikely that any larvae would survive such a process.

Other borers

Although there are many other borers capable of attacking standing trees and green timber, they are unlikely to have the commercial significance of the four types described above. Most of the other groups of borers are exclusively forest insects whose damage does not greatly affect the market value of the timber or end product. Certain bark beetles and weevils sometimes attack the sapwood or the wood immediately under the bark of the tree, and weevils often attack decayed wood. There are species of jewel beetles and wood-boring moths that occasionally bore through into heartwood. None of these insects are very common, however, and although evidence of their work is sometimes apparent, a detailed knowledge of their habits is not considered essential for people other than foresters.

3. Borers attacking dry wood

Powder post borers

The powder post borers are classified in the order Coleoptera and the families Lyctidae and, in some rare cases, Bostrychidae. The lyctids are the most common borers attacking seasoned hardwood in Victoria, so much so that most unprotected susceptible timber is attacked in the first two or three years of service.

The most important fact to remember about these borers is that they attack only the sapwood of certain hardwoods. Because heartwood is never attacked, their attack can cause serious structural weakening only in timbers that have a large sapwood content. Two factors determine the susceptibility of sapwood of the various species of hardwood to lyctid attack. These are the diameter of the pores of the timber and its starch content. Attack is initiated by the female beetle laying her eggs in the pores of susceptible sapwood. If pores of a species are too small to accommodate the ovipositor, then that species will be immune from attack. One or two weeks after oviposition, the eggs hatch into tiny larvae, which bore into and through the sapwood, usually parallel with the grain of the timber, extracting starch for nourishment. If the timber contains insufficient starch, there will be no larval development and such timber may be regarded as immune. The larvae grow as they tunnel, and the galleries become packed with flour-like, powdery frass. In hot climates and artificially heated buildings, the larval period may be as short as three or four months, but in the southern states the normal period of development is 9-12 months. At the end of this time, the fully developed larvae pupate and subsequently emerge from the wood as adult beetles. In emerging, the beetles cut their way out of the wood, leaving a round, unstained emergence hole 1-3 mm in diameter. This may be the first indication of lyctid infestation, as the naked eye cannot see where eggs have been laid in the pores, and all damage is done by the larvae boring below the surface. The powdery frass is often ejected through emergence holes, and it may then collect in small piles on under-lying surfaces. In house framing, frass may continue to be vibrated from old flight holes long after Lyctid attack has died out.

If infested timber has been used in house framing, an adult emerging from a stud or nogging is quite likely to puncture the lining materials. Thus, plaster, hardboard, wallboard or timber lining placed hard against the sapwood of a stud may contain small holes made by adult lyctid borers emerging from the framing beneath. This does not mean, of course, that the linings are sus-ceptible to these or any other borers: merely by being placed hard against the sapwood of a stud, they block the path of emergence and so are cut through by the adult beetle. As emergence holes in lining materials may be unsightly, it is good building practice to install studs, noggings and ceiling joists with the sapwood edge away from the lining.

Adults are small, dark brown beetles 2-6 mm in length. Susceptible sap-wood may be attacked by lyctid borers once the timber dries out to a moisture content of 25-20 per cent. The attack thus often occurs at about the moisture content where the attack of the bostrychid Mesoxylion ceases.

In Queensland and New South Wales, where rain forest timbers, often with very wide sapwoods, are commonly used, legislation regulates the sale of tim-ber susceptible to attack by the lyctid borer and controls the type of treat-ment that may be used to immunize such timber from attack. However, the sale of untreated lyctid-susceptible scantling timber is permitted by the Timber Users' Protection Act in Queensland and the Timber Marketing Act in New South Wales provided not more than one quarter of the perimeter of the piece is in susceptible sapwood. Destruction of this fraction of the cross-section is not likely to cause any serious weakening in structural timbers.

Victorian hardwoods have a comparatively narrow sapwood band, and it is rare for scantlings of Victorian hardwood to contain more than this amount of sapwood. Lyctid attack in framing timbers in Victoria is therefore unlikely to cause structural weakening of any practical importance in a building, so legislation similar to that in force in New South Wales and Queensland is not currently prescribed in Victoria.

Because lyctid eggs are laid in the pores of the timber and not in cracks, crevices etc., timber that has been sealed on its exposed surfaces and ends by paint, varnish, polish or waxes cannot be attacked, because the pores will be blocked. However, if the timber is infested before the application of the finish, adult borers will have no difficulty in emerging through the coating. Once this has occurred, subsequent infestation may occur by re-entry through old emergence holes.

In common with many other borers, lyctids cannot survive the temperatures used in kiln-drying processes. However, this should not be taken to indicate that kiln-dried hardwood is immune from lyctid attack as this is not the case. Kiln-drying does not alter the pore size or the starch content of the timber and therefore cannot affect its susceptibility.

Anobiid borers

There are many different species of anobiid borer, but only four are important enough to warrant the provision of some details. As their habits vary considerably, they will be described separately.

Anobium punctatum

Although Anobium punctatum is commonly known in its native England as the furniture borer, it attacks not only furniture but also flooring, structural timbers and decorative woodwork. This beetle shows a preference for old, well-seasoned timber, and in Australia, its attack is most common in softwoods such as Baltic pine or New Zealand white pine. It is known that A. punctatum will also attack some hardwoods such as blackwood and, in particular, imported hardwoods such as English oak. Australian eucalypts appear to be virtually immune from this destructive insect. Old furniture is frequently attacked, particularly pieces such as pianos, large cupboards etc. Although a high moisture content is not essential for this borer, it does show a preference for rather damp, humid conditions, and attack on flooring is often found to be most severe in those areas of a house where the sub-floor ventilation is inadequate. Probably the most common incidence of domestic A. punctatum attack in Australia is in Baltic pine flooring in older houses with poor sub-floor ventilation and in cupboards and shelving of New Zealand white pine.

Eggs are laid by the female beetle in cracks and crevices in suscpetible timber and also on the rough surface of unprotected end-grain. After two to five weeks, the eggs hatch into larvae, which bore into the timber in a fairly random manner, not necessarily along the grain, attacking both sapwood and heartwood. They produce granular frass of a consistency similar to that of table salt, although the granules tend to be flattened ovals.

In Australia, the larval period lasts from one to three years. After pupation, the adult beetle emerges from the timber, leaving a round, unstained emergence hole similar to that caused by the lyctid borer. Anobiid infestation, which often results in structural weakening, can be far more serious than lyctid attack. Once attack is initiated, it is unlikely to cease or die out of its own accord without some sort of eradicative treatment. Old furniture that has been in store or has been obtained from auction rooms may be infested, and if taken to a house where there is susceptible softwood timber, the infestation may spread. However, because it spreads slowly, it can be controlled in furniture before the damage becomes too serious.

The adult is a small, dark brown to charcoal-coloured beetle, usually 3-5 mm long.

Calymmaderus incisus

The Queensland pine beetle, as Calymmaderus incisus is commonly known, is an anobiid that in Queensland frequently attacks softwood timbers, predominantly hoop pine and, less frequently, bunya pine and New Zealand white pine. It has not been recorded as occurring in other states, but this may be because it has very similar habits to A. punctatum, has a similar life-cycle and causes similar damage, and both larvae and adults are very similar in appearance to the furniture beetle. Experience in Queensland has shown that C. incisus attack is generally initiated in the darker sub-floor areas and that it subsequently spreads by the re-infestation of later generations.

Ernobius mollis

Ernobius mollis, a species of anobiid, is a cambium borer of softwoods and, as such, its damage is rarely of any great importance. However, since it is often mistaken for the furniture beetle A. punctatum, some information on its habits and peculiarities may help to avoid confusion.

The female beetle lays her eggs in the bark of softwoods. The larvae can breed only if bark is present, although damage may spread into the outer sapwood. Because E. mollis does not attack living trees or green timber and is not a forest insect, and because it can only attack dry timber that still has bark on it, the borer is not a common pest. In localities where softwood building scantlings are in general use, the possibility of dry softwood with some bark present is very real, and this timber is susceptible to E. mollis attack. The frass produced by this borer is gritty, and because the insect attacks both bark and cambium, it is usually speckled, as some grains are from the bark and others from the lighter cambium or sapwood.

A more common source of E. mollis attack is the bark around knots in softwood. The insect can be present in and subsequently emerge from wood surrounding the knot.

Eradicative treatment is not usually necessary apart from stripping the bark from the timber, after which attack will cease. If nothing is done at all, an attack will often die out within a few years either because the food supply has run out or because the bark has simply fallen off.

Anobium australiense

Anobium australiense attacks both softwoods and hardwoods, but only when conditions are conductive to decay. The adult beetle is similar in form to the furniture borer Anobium punctatum but is about twice the size (7-8 mm) and rather darker, being almost black. The emergence holes are round and unstained like those of the furniture borer, although they are appreciably larger. Attack is often confined to sapwood, but when heartwood has been softened by decay, attack will spread to it also. The frass produced by the larvae is powdery, looks dirty and tends to be packed in the tunnels by the moisture that is usually associated with the decay. Once the moist conditions conducive to decay have been removed and the decay arrested, the attack ceases.

The dry wood longicorns (cerambycids)

Normally, longicorn or cerambycid beetles initiate attack in green timber and, although they may complete their life-cycle in, and emerge from, timber that has been allowed to dry naturally, they cannot re-infest dry timber. There are, however, very few beetles of this family that are able to initiate attack in dry wood and to cause serious damage to it. Fortunately, none of these exceptions occurs naturally in Australia, although there have been instances of them being imported into Australia in timber from abroad.

Hylotrupes bajulus

Hylotrupes bajulus, a cerambycid beetle, is common in many parts of Europe, the United States and South Africa. In the United Kingdom, it is known as the house longhorn beetle, in Germany as the Hausbock, in France as the capricorne des maisons, in the United States as the old house borer, and throughout the rest of the world as the European house borer. All these names imply that housing timbers are frequently attacked by this pest, and indeed this is so. Because it can attack and infest seasoned softwood, it has become a pest of major importance in those countries where it has become established. It attacks softwoods such as pine, fir and spruce and so thoroughly excavates the timber that it causes severe structural damage. Hardwoods are not attacked by H. bajulus.

Although its average life-cycle in Europe is from three to six years, the beetle can live ten years or more. Some softwood timbers, infested in Europe and subsequently imported into Australia, have had adult H. bajulus emerge more than 10 years after their arrival here. Many hundreds of pre-fabricated houses imported by various government departments shortly after the Second World War have been thoroughly inspected and, where necessary, fumigated with methyl bromide. As far as is known, such measures have prevented this most dangerous of all longicorns from becoming established in Australia.

The adult beetle may vary in length from 6 to 25 mm. Its overall colour is greyish-brown to black, with light patches on the wing covers.

Ambeodontus tristis

The two-toothed longicorn, as Ambeodontus tristis is frequently called, is a native of New Zealand. This beetle attacks dry New Zealand rimu and some pines. Like the European house borer, it has been found in imported timber in Australia but it has not become established here.

The adult beetle varies in length from 6 to 25 mm and is a uniform brown colour.

4. Methods of control

Predators and parasites

In nature, most insect pests are limited in number either by birds or by other insects, and wood borers are no exception to this. Adults of forest borers such as those attacking standing trees and green timber are frequently eaten by birds, and sometimes the larvae may be extracted from the tree by birds pecking through bark to reach them. However, there are other insects whose primary function is to parasitize various stages of certain wood-boring species.

In Australia, the most common and active predators of wood-boring beetles are those of the family Cleridae. The various clerid species are predatory in both their larval and adult forms, and some of them attack most of the borers previously mentioned in this chapter, including pinholes, longicorns and bostrychids in the forest and lyctids in dry wood. A very common species, Paratillus carus, lays its eggs in the sapwood of hardwood that has already been infested by lyctids. After hatching, the long, thin larvae move around in the wood, using galleries made by lyctid larvae, and when one of these is encountered, it is killed and devoured. The adults of P. carus are larger than those of lyctids, being up to 8 mm long, and are easily distinguished by a white band across the wing covers, giving this species the common name of the white-banded clerid. These adults are predacious on adult lyctid beetles and often decapitate them.

Another familiar predator is the yellow-horned clerid, Trogodendron fasciculatum, adults of which may be seen flying in the daytime or resting on trees or timber in the open. This species is predacious on both the larvae and adults of many species of longicorn: the larvae kill longicorn larvae and the adults kill longicorn adults. The adult Trogodendron is often 25 mm or more in length and will fearlessly attack longicorn adults much larger than itself. If picked up in the hand, it may bite the finger and be rather hard to dislodge.

In addition to the clerids, there are a number of wasps that are predators of wood borers at the larval stage. Two such wasps, Rhyssa spp. and Ibalia spp., have recently been imported into Victoria, because they are predators upon the larvae of the sirex wood wasp. Other parasites of the sirex species include the nematodes, which can breed in the gut and therefore parasitize larvae and adults. Also, various species of mites, particularly the hay-itch mite Pyemotes ventriculosis, obtain their nourishment from the larvae of both lyctid and anobiid borers in dry wood.

While predatory parasites do have some control over the wood-boring population, they are not sufficiently numerous to prevent borer infestation in susceptible timbers. It is therefore necessary to use other methods of control: either chemical treatments or the selection on non-susceptible timber species.

Treatment before use

Numerous insecticidal formulations have been used, with varying degrees of success and persistence, to protect logs and green sawn timber from borer attack. Seasoned timber may be immunized (permanently protected) against borer attack by fully impregnating the susceptible wood with a preservative that does not deteriorate and that is not lost from the wood during its service life.

It is often economical to prevent lyctid attack by removing susceptible sapwood from the timber.

Treatment of lyctid borers

For building timbers, pressure impregnation or, more frequently, hot immersion or steam and cold quench treatments are used. The boron or fluorine compounds that are commonly used in these treatments are very effective in preventing lyctid attack but do not become fixed in the wood as do the metal-chrome-arsenic waterborne preservatives and can therefore be leached out if wetted.

Spraying hardwood house frames against lyctid attack is of no value. In general, all unprotected susceptible sapwood is likely to become infested with lyctid borer within the first few summers of service and any timbers not attacked after about five years are, in all probability, immune from attack. Spraying is a surface treatment only and has little or no effect on any larvae inside the wood; once the house is completed, effective retreatment of all timbers is virtually impossible.

The fact that woodwork has been attacked by borers is usually not apparent until after the building is completed. Where only limited sapwood is present, treatment against lyctid attack is rarely necessary for structural reasons, but unless treatment is given as soon as the holes first appear, an attack in finishing timbers may mar their appearance.

Treatment of anobiid borers

Anobiid attack does require treatment. Insecticides such as aldrin, dieldrin, chlordane, heptachlor, DDT etc. in a light oil solvent such as mineral turpentine or kerosine can be used against borers in seasoned timber. It may be applied by syringe through finished surfaces into emergence holes and forced in until the timber is saturated. Penetration is improved by removing loose frass from galleries with a vacuum cleaner before treatment. Once the insecticide has dried, the holes may be plugged and the surface finish restored. On timbers with unfinished surfaces, the insecticide should be liberally applied with a brush so as to get as much into the timber as possible. This applies particularly to the underside of softwood flooring that has been infested with anobiids.

Fumigation

Fumigation is a treatment used only in special cases, usually for individual packages of timber or pieces of furniture. It involves placing the items in an air-tight compartment, e.g. a cylinder, a special room or under polythene tarpaulins, and pumping a liquid fumigant into the area. The fumigant, often methyl bromide, vapourizes, and the resultant gas permeates through timber and destroys any adults, pupae, larvae or eggs that may be present. Although fumigation kills any pest in the timber at the time of fumigation, it cannot be described as a preservative treatment as it confers no immunity from subsequent attack. It is commonly used for the treatment of imported timber known to contain foreign pests, of individual pieces of infested furniture and occasionally for entire houses that are known to contain timber infested with borers that are subject to quarantine regulations. This operation, however, is a very expensive one and is used only in exceptional circumstances.

Quarantine control

The Commonwealth Department of Health administers plant quarantine in Australia, and its duties are carried out in the various states by special officers of the local Department of Agriculture.

All timber entering Australia is subject to quarantine inspection and control. The timber arrives in the form of green logs, sawn timber, furniture and other manufactured articles as well as in the form of packaging timbers and dunnage. Quarantine regulations are such that if any evidence of borer attack is present in imported timber, the timber is either compulsorily fumigated at the expense of the consignee or else it is destroyed. The importation of bark or timber containing bark is prohibited. The more quarantine-conscious timber importers and timber users become, the more successful will be the task of keeping the country free from overseas pests and the more sound will be the future of the Australian timber trade.

It is often argued that except where prohibitions are rigidly enforced, or where the climate serves to control the pest population, a quarantine system cannot expect to succeed indefinitely and that, gradually, many of its barriers will be penetrated. This may be true, but it does not alter the fact that as long as there are diseases or pests that can be excluded, a quarantine service is of immense value, and that it is the obligation of every person to abide by its regulations.

As a matter of principle, the timber trade and timber-using industries must realize that no quarantine system can function effectively if avoidable risks are taken. Vested interests must not be allowed to affect policy or influence the setting of standards for safety. The need for an uncompromising attitude in quarantine matters is not always appreciated, though on reflection it should be obvious that a risk taken only once or a mistake made only once may cause irreparable harm on a national level and nullify all the vigilance of the past. Because of this there are good reasons - technical, economic and psychological - for the strict enforcement of regulations and decisions that, if regarded individually, may seem unduly stringent or arbitrary. In some cases there may even be justification for applying such regulations on the basis of suspicion alone.

C. Wood-destroying insects: termites

1. Occurrence and distribution

Termites, or "white ants", are to be found in most tropical countries and are widely distributed in temperate regions. Australia has its fair share of these insects, with over 300 different species having been recognized and described, and few parts of the continent or surrounding islands are without them.

Termites are among the few insects capable of utilizing cellulose as a source of food. Since cellulose is the major constituent of most plant tissues, most plants and plant products are likely to be susceptible to termite damage. Under natural conditions, termites of one sort or another feed on the roots of grasses, living trees, dry wood or decaying vegetable matter. However, when given the opportunity, they may also damage or destroy paper, building boards, linoleum, leather and bone. Even buried telephone cables, plastic waterpipes and the lagging around steam pipes have been known to suffer from termite attack. Thus, wherever they occur, some termite species are likely to damage or destroy articles useful to man, and precautions must be taken to minimize the losses they might cause.

The old adage "Prevention is better than cure" applies as much to termite attack as to anything else. New buildings can be given permanent protection against termite attack by including suitable barriers in the structure during construction, while timbers of low natural resistance can be given immunity from attack by means of preservative treatments. The cost of such precautions generally represents only a very small fraction of the total cost of the structures they protect. To take precautions is good insurance; to ignore them in areas of unknown or high hazard is seldom wise.

2. Identification of ants and termites

Ants (Hymenoptera) and termites (Isoptera) - the latter are commonly called white ants - are two orders of insects that have many characteristics in common. Both contain a large number of species and live in colonies or organized communities whose members are divided into castes of more or less specialized individuals. The differences between the two groups of insects are numerous, obvious and fairly consistent, but because of variations among species or castes within a species, it may be necessary to examine and compare several individuals before making an identification. In figure 1 and table 2, the differences between ants and soldier caste termites are noted.

Figure 1. Anatomy of an ant and a soldier caste termite

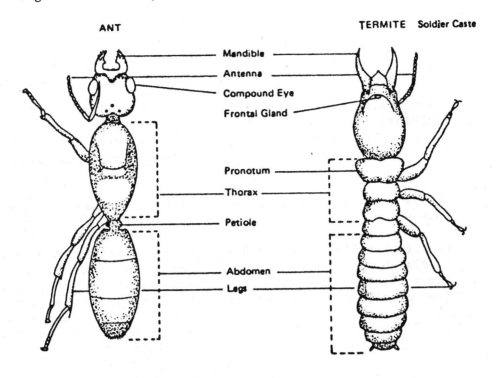

Table 2. Differences between ants and termites

Character-istics	Ants	Termites
Antenna	"Elbowed", first segment always long, about as long as the head.	Never elbowed; 11 to 15 segments long, like a string of beads.
Mandible	Terminates in cutting edge, never pointed.	If visible, terminates in a point.
Compound eye	Always present, obvious.	Absent except in winged forms. Simple _ocelli_ (eyes) sometimes present.
Neck	Distinct and thin.	Not obvious.
Thorax	Distinct, large, often equal to or larger than abdomen.	Inconspicuous, three distinct segments. Seldom bigger than the head, never as large as abdomen.
Legs	Long, usually able to reach past head and tail.	Short. Incapable of reaching to end of abdomen.
Petiole	Always present; 1, 2 or 3 segments forming "waist".	Never present.

continued

Table 2 (<u>continued</u>)

Character-istics	Ants	Termites
Abdomen	Often small, compact and globular; carried well off ground. Generally 3-5 indistinct segments.	Large, usually more than half total length of body. Soft, usually rests on ground. Always seven or more segments, fairly distinct.
Anal end	Always ends in a point. May have sting.	Blunt or obtuse. Never has a sting.
Colour	Usually heavily pigmented dark reddish-brown to black; some-times lighter, orangy thorax. Head usually about as dark as body.	Always light, creamy or pearly, but stomach contents may give some species a smoky colour. Head may be same as body or, in soldier caste, pigmented yellow, orange to dark brown with darker mandibles.
Toughness	Strong-bodied, well-adapted to foraging in open.	Soft-bodied, easily squashed, ill-adapted to survive in the open.
Speed in the open	Brisk, often run faster than 1.5 m per minute.	Comparatively sluggish, do not run. Approximate speed 0.5 m/min.
Runways or trails	May follow trails in the open. Do not build covered shelter-tubes but may invade and occupy tunnels excavated by other insects. Commonly found for-aging freely in the open.	Never found foraging freely out-side their galleries or runway systems but do move freely within the enclosed galleries of the system.
When disturbed	Scurry frantically in all directions, making no attempt to hide. Many species bite or sting viciously.	Immediately attempt to escape and find shelter away from bright lights, heat or draughts. Do not sting. Bite (if any) is barely perceptible on the thin skin between fingers.
Odour	Generally have strong pungent odour when crushed.	Practically odourless when crushed.
"Poison"	Never eject milky fluid from head but may have poison gland associated with sting in the tail.	Soldiers of certain species may eject droplet of milky fluid from head.
Damage caused in wood	Do not attack wood. May estab-lish temporary nests in wall cavities, between pairs of studs or in other narrow spaces.	Attack may not be detected until extensive damage has occurred. Later stages of attack, interior of wood is eaten away to leave only a paper-thin surface veneer.

3. Termite classification

Correct identification of the different species of termites requires considerable skill and experience. Fortunately, a detailed identification is seldom necessary when dealing with species of economic importance to wood-using industries. Within broad limits and with the clear understanding that some species might be correctly placed in more than one group, figure 2 offers a simple classification based upon habits. This classification serves to segregate the different types or groups of species that are of economic importance and emphasizes the characteristics of the few species that are of direct concern to the timber user. In fact, only the tree-dwelling species and the subterranean termites are of major economic importance to the timber industry.

Figure 2. Classification of termites

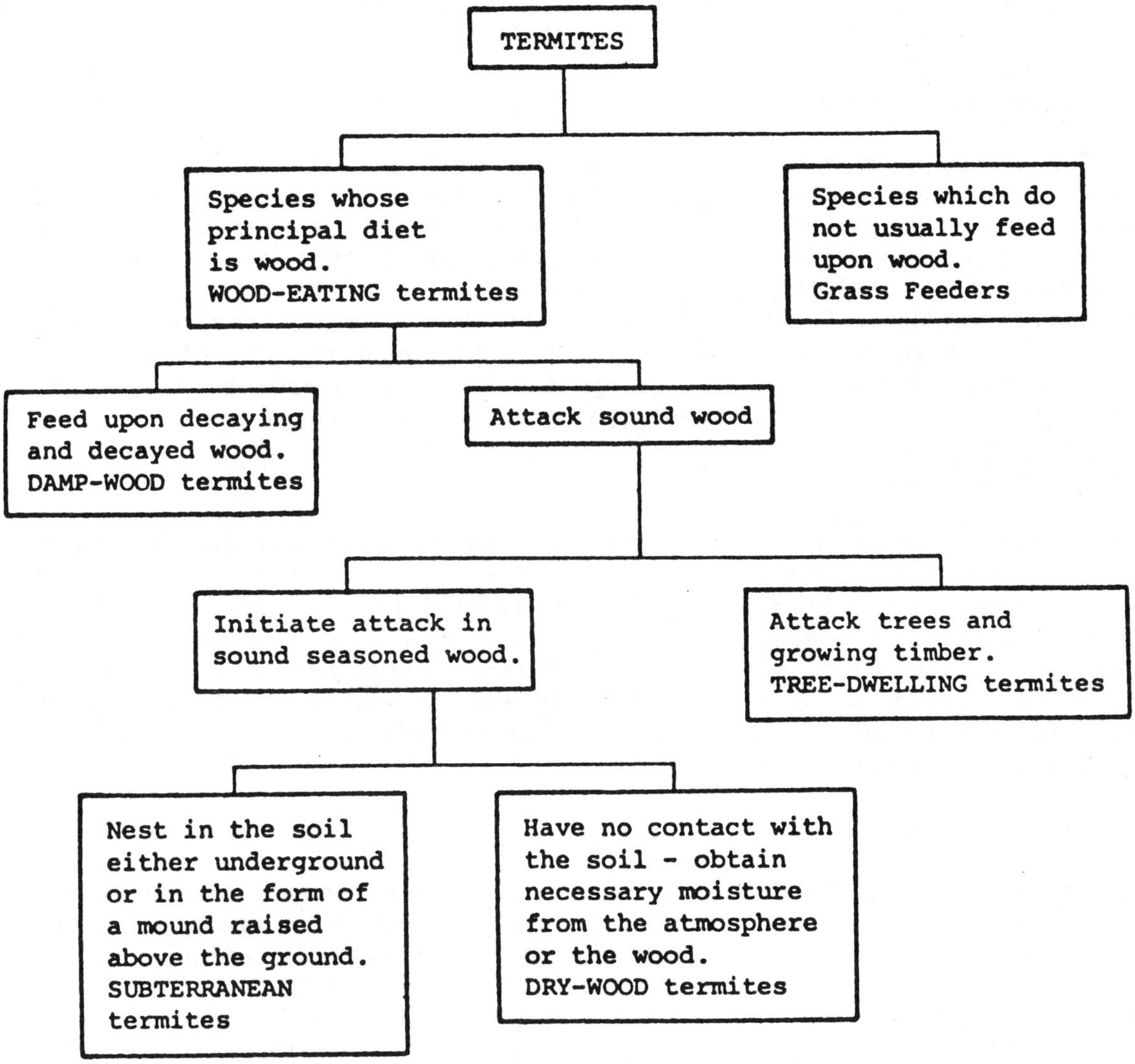

Ratcliffe, Gay and Greaves [2] suggest that the term subterranean termite should be reserved for those forms that nest underground or near ground level in a treep stump, log or post and should not include those forms that construct an exposed nest or mound. For the purposes of this discussion, the difference is immaterial and the term subterranean will include both forms.

4. Important termite species

Damp-wood species

Damp-wood species are always associated with rotting wood, usually in the form of fallen logs in the forest but also sometimes decayed wood in buildings, fences etc. Usually the decay precedes the termite attack.

Stolotermes victoriensis

Stolotermes victoriensis, a termite of variable size, is sometimes mistaken for Neotermes insularis or Porotermes adamsomi because of its size. The soldiers, which are fairly numerous in the colonies, are 6-11 mm long and are easily recognized by their extremely flattened heads and their pointed, leaf-like mandibles, which do not show a marked upward or downward curve when seen in profile. The pronotum is very much narrower than the head. Small but distinct eyes are usually present in the soldiers.

Porotermes adamsoni

Porotermes adamsoni is most commonly found as a forest pest. It causes considerable damage to standing trees, particularly in cooler localities. Found in fallen logs in an advanced state of decay, it is probable that the attack originated in the standing tree, indicating that the colony and, perhaps, some of the individuals of the colony are very long-lived. Porotermes, although primarily a forest pest, does attack timber in service and has been found in a variety of situations attacking hardwood timbers of many species, including some of the more durable species used for house stumps; in all such cases, however, the termite attack can be traced back to decayed wood.

Tree-dwelling species

Attack by tree-dwelling termites may be of considerable concern to the forester, the timber-getter or the sawmiller but is seldom of much importance to the timber-user. In general, timber damaged by tree-dwelling termites is discarded during conversion and very little evidence of the damage reaches the consumer. Occasionally, small pockets of termite-damaged wood containing a few live insects might be present in freshly sawn scantlings. These few insects will soon die without causing further damage because they are isolated from their supply of moisture and their parent colony.

Neotermes insularis

Essentially a forest pest, Neotermes insularis shows a marked tendency to attack growing trees through wounds at some distance above ground. It may then work downward through the centre of the log. Attack may continue in the sound wood of fallen logs, but it is believed that this would have been initiated when the tree was standing. On the basis of the soldier caste, it is the largest termite, with soldiers from 9 to 15 mm long. Soldiers of N. insularis may be distinguished from those of Porotermes by the following characteristics:

(a) The pronotum is as wide as the head;

(b) The head is not noticeably flattened;

(c) The mandibles are long and, seen in profile, have an upward curve.

Soldiers of N. insularis vary greatly in size and in the size and profile of their mandibles.

Subterranean species

In addition to the obvious damage to timber in service, subterranean species may also attack growing trees and cause a significant reduction in the volume of millable wood that can be recovered from their trunks. They are both a forest pest and a pest of seasoned timber.

Coptotermes

Three species, Coptotermes acinaciformis, C. frenchi and C. lacteus, are common. Since it is not easy to distinguish between these species and since they have similar habits, they may be treated collectively as the most economically important group of termites in the country. Coptotermes attack both trees and seasoned timber. Their nests may be completely underground, in an old stump or a living tree or in the form of a domed or rounded conical mound, which may rise several feet above ground. Soldiers are smallish, up to about 6 mm long, and have rounded, rather pear-shaped, yellowish heads and dark slender tapering mandibles without visible teeth. Their habit of exuding a drop of milky fluid from the frontal gland when disturbed or annoyed offers a sure means of identifying them in life. Soldiers are relatively numerous in the colonies and when the galleries are broken open will usually appear after a short interval.

Nasutitermes exitiosus

Nasutitermes exitiosus attacks seasoned timber, poles, posts and sawn timber. It is a mould-building species that adopts its nesting habits to local conditions. Under natural conditions, its mound may be built around or over a stump or piece of wood in which, presumably, the colony was originally founded. When it attacks buildings, the nest is likely to conform to the shape of the wall cavity or the sub-floor space available.

5. Termite biology

Ancestry

Fossil records show that the progenitors of modern termites date back more than 50 million years and that termites and cockroaches have a common ancestry. In fact, the wing structure of the most primitive living termite, Mastotermes darwiniensis, the giant termite of tropical Australia, is similar to that of the roaches, and its egg mass resembles the egg-capsule of the roaches. As further evidence of a common ancestry for roaches and termites, one roach burrows into the sounder wood of decaying logs for food and shelter and, like Mastotermes and many other groups of termites, has a rich protozoan or bacterial fauna in its gut to aid in the digestion of its food.

Biological limitations

The biology of the termites is interesting and complex, but only those aspects of termite biology that are relevant to the control of attack by subterranean termites will be discussed here. Although the observations will be in general terms, this limitation should not be overlooked.

Life span

The life span of the individuals in a termite colony is believed to be as much as 25 years for the reproductive castes but considerably less for the other castes. Certainly, there is no difficulty in maintaining a laboratory colony of sterile workers and soldiers for a period of four years or so.

The life span of the colony varies with the species, assuming there is no untoward accident to interrupt its development. With some species it is believed that the original pair of reproductives that founded the colony are never replaced or supplanted. If this is so, the life span of the colony is limited to that of the founding pair, plus the limited period for which the remaining members of the colony will survive without further replacements. With species capable of producing supplementary reproductives, which either supplement the original queen or, if she suffers an accident or dies, replace her, the life of the colony is indefinite and might well exceed a century or two.

Industry

Termites are industrious. It is virtually impossible to observe them under natural conditions without disturbing or disrupting the colony. In laboratory colonies, the constant activity of these insects is amazing, and there is no reason to suppose that they are less active under natural conditions. It should be recognized, however, that activity tends to be reduced in cold weather and that foraging may cease altogether during spells of hot dry weather.

Moisture and light

There is a common belief that subterranean termites must return to water once in every 24 hours. This may be true for some species, but it is certainly not universally true.

Apart from the colonizing flight of the reproductive castes, subterranean termites spend the whole of their existence in the galleries and tunnels associated with their nest.

Conditions in these galleries and tunnels, and the nest, are uniform and fairly constant. Total darkness prevails at all times, humidities are high and diurnal temperature fluctuations are minimized. Termites have become so specialized that these are virtually the only conditions they can now tolerate. Since their activities are confined to a gallery system in which the relative humidity is always high, their integument (outer covering, or "skin") does not need to be a good moisture barrier. In fact, it is very permeable, so that when termites are exposed to a dry atmosphere they lose moisture and soon die from desiccation. Also, the surface of their bodies is normally moist. Thus, any dry dust particles with which they might come in contact adhere, only to be removed when the insects groom one another.

Living in total darkness, termites have largely lost the faculty of sight and most of them are either blind or almost so. Being perpetually sheltered from normal light and radiation, termites have little need of pigmentation as a filter against ultraviolet light. Hence, their integument is either trans-lucent or very poorly pigmented, except for the head and jaws of the soldier caste, which tend to be hard and horny and to contain more pigmentation.

Protein conservation

The plant tissues upon which termites feed contain very little protein. Hence it is reasonable to assume that a termite colony needs some mechanism for the conservation of protein. It has been suggested that termites conserve their protein by (a) cannibalism and (b) grooming.

There is a considerable amount of evidence to support the contention that termites dispose of dead and diseased members of the colony by cannibalism and some evidence to suggest that surplus or unwanted members may suffer a similar fate. Certainly such a procedure would be a convenient and efficient method of protein conservation.

It is well known that termites groom one another. This may be because their bodies lack the flexibility necessary for them to be able to clean themselves and this duty must be delegated to other members of the colony, but it is also quite evident that their body secretions are attractive to other members of the colony and are eagerly sought after. This habit of grooming is of prime importance in termite control work. If a poison dust such as finely divided white arsenic powder is blown into occupied termite galleries, it will be fairly widely distributed by the initial blast. It will also adhere to the rather moist bodies of any insects that come in contact with it. This will aid and extend its distribution. Since termites habitually groom each other, the particles of poison will be ingested along with other body secretions, with the inevitable result. The poison remains active in the dead bodies and, if these are eaten, it continues to kill.

Digestion and food preferences

Termites show considerable discrimination in their choice of food. If subterranean termites, which normally feed upon wood, are given a free choice between two timbers, they preferentially will consume the more susceptible of the two. Several timbers are seldom attacked by termites under natural conditions, but in compulsion tests, where the termites have the choice between eating the resistant species or starving, few timbers are totally immune from their attack.

In Victoria, subterranean termites normally feed upon hardwoods. The Nasutitermes species found there practically never attack softwoods, but the Coptotermes species show no such discrimination.

Social organization

Termites are social insects that usually live in large, populous colonies that may contain over a million individuals. Activities within the colony appear to be divided between groups of specialized members, referred to as castes. The population of a mature colony of subterranean termites will consist of three principal castes and juvenile forms. The three major castes are the reproductives, the soldiers and the workers. For various reasons, classification of the different species is based upon the morphology of the soldier caste.

Reproductives

Reproductives are the only members of the colony to be complete with appendages, including eyes and wings, and functional reproductive parts. Once their colonizing flight is completed, they shed their wings and as first-form reproductives - or first-form kings and queens - set about founding a new colony. A first-form queen can practically always be recognized by her wing stubs and her distended abdomen, which, in Nasutitermes, for example, may become so enlarged that she is several hundred times the size of a soldier or a worker.

Some species produce additional reproductives to help populate the colony and to replace the original queen if she is injured. These remain permanently in the mother colony, though not necessarily in the central nest. In fact, they may found a new colony by a process of budding off. As the strength of the daughter colony increases, communication with the parent colony may be lost and the new colony may become independent.

As a colony matures, it produces reproductives that, when weather conditions are suitable, leave the parent colony in swarms in an attempt to found new colonies. These swarms of "flying ants" usually emerge from close to the parent colony and may be of some help in finding the site of the nest.

The reproductives are the only termites that leave the shelter of the gallery system, and this happens only during their brief colonizing flight, after which they seek a suitable site in which to found a new colony. Fortunately, of the millions that set out, only an occasional pair succeeds.

Juvenile reproductives, or nymphs, may be recognized by the presence of wing buds and, sometimes, by their larger size.

Soldiers

Apparently the main function of soldiers is to defend the colony against ants, one of the termites' principal enemies. The soldiers are most useful in termite classification and should always be procured if a species is to be identified. Soldiers may be recognized by their dark-coloured heads and, if closely examined, well-developed mandibles (except in Nasutitermes, which has a pear-shaped head).

Workers

In nearly all species, workers constitute the great majority of the inhabitants of a colony. They are uniformly pale-coloured, with rounded heads and soft bodies, and are blind and sterile.

6. Prevention of termite attack

Whenever doubt exists as to the adequacy of the precautions proposed for the prevention of termite attack in buildings or other structures in which wood has been used, the proposals should be checked by specialists before any work commences so that modifications can be made with a minimum of inconvenience.

It should be noted that the precautions described apply to conditions in Victoria, where subterranean termites are responsible for practically all the damage of economic consequence to timber in service. In other states, alternative methods may be more acceptable.

Timber in the ground

When timber is used in the ground, as poles, posts, railway ties or house foundations, soil-dwelling termites have direct access to it. Commonly, their foraging galleries lie from 100 to 200 mm below the surface of the soil and attack is usually initiated at about this level. However, in dry soils it is by no means rare for attack to be initiated at a much greater depth.

Resistant timbers

The heartwood of a number of eucalypt timbers is very resistant to termite attack without any form of preservative treatment. Resistant timbers at Victoria, Australia, are shown in table 3.

Table 3. Resistant timbers at Victoria, Australia

Durability class	Standard trade or common name	Botanical name
1	Box, grey	_E. microcarpa_ (Maid.)
	Box, grey, coast	_E. bosistoana_ F. Muell.
	Ironbark, red	_E. sideroxylon_ A. Cunn.
2	Gum, red, forest	_E. tereticornis_ Sm.
	Gum, red, river	_E. camaldulensis_ Dehnh.
	Gum, yellow	_E. leucoxylon_ F. Muell.
	Stringybark, white	_E. eugenioides_ Sieb.
	Stringybark, yellow	_E. muelleriana_ Howitt

Impregnated timber

Only the sapwood of most hardwood timbers can be impregnated with wood preservatives by conventional methods. Therefore, unless the species is one of those listed as resistant, the benefits of preservation will be lost unless all the sapwood is intact. With softwood timbers, particularly _P. radiata_, which normally have a comparatively wide sapwood band, at least 80 per cent of the cross-section should be fully and uniformly penetrated.

AS 1604-1974, Preservative-Treated Sawn Timber, Veneer and Plywood, and AS 2209-1979, Timber Poles for Overhead Lines, both deal with the preservative treatment of timber used in ground contact.

AS 1604-1974 relates the penetration and retention of wood preservative to the natural durability of the timber species and to the anticipated hazards of service. Appendices to this Standard deal with the composition of commercial wood preservatives available in Australia, the sampling and testing of preservatives and preservative-treated wood, the natural durability of Australian commercial timbers and similar matters. The Standard should be consulted for the recommended retentions of commercial preservatives in various classes of timber for any particular end use.

Soil puddling

Sawn heartwood and other impermeable timbers can be given a useful measure of protection against subterranean termite attack by surrounding them with an annulus, or collar, of soil thoroughly mixed with a persistent insecticide. To be effective, this collar must be in direct contact with the timber to be protected, not less than 50 mm wide (measured radially from the surface of the wood) and extending for at least 0.5 m below ground level. In dry soils it may be necessary to carry the collar down deeper.

The persistent insecticides allowed in AS 2057-1977, Soil Treatment for the Protection of Buildings against Subterranean Termites, will also be found effective for protecting timber in ground contact against termite attack but not against decay. They are usually purchased as emulsifiable concentrates and applied as diluted emulsions at the rate of about 150 $1/m^3$ of soil.

Timber in buildings

With buildings, it is necessary to protect the contents of a building from damage by termites as much as to preserve the structure itself. In fact, the contents of a shop or warehouse often exceed the value of the building. Therefore, protection against termite attack is just as necessary in a building in which all the materials of construction are immune from termite damage as in one built entirely of timber. Normally, termites forage in concealed tunnels beneath the surface of the soil or in galleries in the timber they attack. However, they will build mud-covered shelter tubes over materials they cannot penetrate in order to reach susceptible timber at some distance above ground. It is by means of these shelter tubes that they gain access to the superstructure of a building or its contents.

Buildings are usually protected against termite attack by mechanical barriers (termite shields, ant caps) placed on top of the foundations or by barriers of chemically treated soil at ground level. In either case the barriers must be continuous and complete so that all possible routes of entry to the building from the soil are intercepted by a barrier. Even then, under some circumstances, termites will raise a mound or a free-standing shelter tube to bypass the barriers. Hence, in areas of established termite hazard, periodic sub-floor inspections are a necessary part of termite protection.

Mechanical termite barriers

When set into continuous foundations, mechanical termite barriers are known as strip shields, but when set over stumps or piers, as caps or ant-caps. Collectively they may be referred to as either capping or shielding. Both are made from galvanized iron of heavier gauge than 26-gauge or from copper.

Correctly made, they should project beyond the foundation they protect before turning downwards. All joints should be carefully mitred and well soldered or spot-welded at close intervals. Detailed instructions for the correct method of fitting shields to buildings are set out and illustrated in AS 1694-1974, Physical Barriers Used in the Protection of Buildings against Subterranean Termites. Because of the need for periodic inspections and because it is very rare to find all the joints and corners properly made, shields are practically never recommended for use in buildings with continuous foundation walls. Hence, their use is more or less restricted to the capping of stumps or piers in timber-framed houses under which inspection presents no difficulty. For ease of inspection, the edges of the shields should stand clear of all obstructions by at least 50 mm.

Treated soil barriers

These may be referred to as chemical barriers. AS 2057-1977 is a code of practice for forming barriers of chemically treated soil as a protection for buildings against subterranean termite attack. This code describes the correct method of forming these barriers, nominates chemicals and concentrations and suggests building modifications that can simplify and reduce the cost of termite prevention. The common chemicals recommended for these barriers are aldrin, dieldrin, chlordane and heptachlor. They are usually used in the form of water emulsions. The treating solution should be applied to the whole of the sub-floor area after it has been cleared of all debris and reasonably levelled. Special attention must be given to areas of fill under concrete slabs raised to the same level as suspended timber floors.

Treated soil barriers are the preferred treatment for concrete raft (slab-on-ground) construction.

7. Eradication of termite attack

The eradication of termite attack is covered in AS 2178-1978, Treatment of Subterranean Termite Infestation in Existing Buildings. In the event that active termite attack is discovered in an existing building, the insects should be left undisturbed until all the materials necessary for treatment have been assembled or arrangements have been completed for treatment by a specialist.

One of the most effective treatments for an active termite infestation is dusting with arsenic dust. Government regulations make it difficult for ordinary householders to obtain this poison, so it is now usual to employ professionals who are licensed to handle poisons. The success of this method depends upon the termites continuing to occupy treated galleries after the dust has been blown in. It is for this reason that a warning is given against disturbing the termites until arrangements for treatment have been completed.

As an alternative to the poison dust treatment recommended in the Standard, the superstructure of the building can be isolated by a barrier of treated soil. If it is formed correctly and it completely surrounds all the foundations, it will protect the building from further attack but may not be effective in eliminating the nest or colony from which the attack originated. Care must also be taken to avoid encircling the termite colony within the treated soil barrier and isolating it from alternative sources of food. This is most likely to happen when the treated soil barrier is formed around a concrete slab that is part of the house.

D. Wood preservatives

Introduction

Wood has many advantages over competing materials for both structural and ornamental uses. Timber does not deteriorate as a result of aging alone: any failure is invariably the result of attack by some external agency, and if adequately protected against dampness, insects, fungal infection and fire, it will, unless exposed to severe mechanical wear, last almost indefinitely.

To some extent the reputation of timber has suffered as a result of deterioration due to attack by fungi or insects. Such biological attack can now be almost entirely prevented, but the preservative measures require a clear understanding of the nature of the organisms concerned; the factors governing their development; the properties of the various timber species and the principles upon which scientific control is based.

Conventionally, timbers have been classified into four durability classes according to the relative natural resistance of their heartwood to biological attack when service conditions involve contact with the ground. It will be realized, however, that in the countless uses of timber that do not involve contact with the ground, for example, weatherboards, joinery and furniture, these ratings have much less significance. There are numerous instances where timber in favourable, protected situations has remained sound and serviceable for generations without having been given any special preservative treatment. However, to ensure long life under conditions of high hazard, it is necessary to use either the more highly durable species or timber of lower natural durability that has been given the recommended preservative treatment.

Decay increases the susceptibility of wood to attack by termites and other wood-boring insects. Indeed, there are many insects that cannot initiate attack in sound, seasoned wood but that can be very destructive to wood in which some decay is present. The damage caused by insects that initiate attack in sound, seasoned wood can be controlled, or entirely prevented, by the use of appropriate preservative treatments or other suitable precautions.

Almost invariably, the sapwood of a timber is less resistant to decay and insect attack than its heartwood. Conversely, the sapwood is nearly always more amenable to preservative treatment than the heartwood. Species vary widely in the natural resistance of their timber to fungal and insect attack. With appropriate preservative treatment, sapwood of practically all species and heartwood of permeable species can be rendered highly resistant to both insect and fungal attack. Thus, with proper preservative treatment, species of low natural resistance may be substituted for timbers of the highest natural durability and may even outperform them.

The prime purpose of any wood preservation process is to extend the useful life of timber in service. This may be achieved by increasing its resistance to damage by invading organisms (fungi, insects or marine animals) or by increasing its resistance to deterioration caused by weathering and other physical forces.

To be effective, preservation processes need to place an adequate quantity of an appropriate preservative far enough into the timber to ensure that no unprotected or insufficiently treated wood becomes accessible to the invading organism or is exposed to other destructive forces.

Numerous methods of treatment have been developed to protect timber against unwanted deterioration. The simplest have required only the application of surface barriers, e.g. paint, coatings of other materials, metal sheathing etc., which are intended to deny moisture and other destructive agencies access to the wood. Other, more sophisticated methods of treatment are designed to distribute through the wood preservative chemicals that are toxic to wood-destroying organisms. Current worldwide research aims at refining these treatment methods and improving the environmental acceptability and other properties of the preservatives to the point where there is a satisfactory preservative and treatment process for practically every normal requirement.

Numerous chemicals and mixtures of chemicals can be used as wood preservatives. Some, like creosote oil and the copper-chrome-arsenic (CCA) salts, are general-purpose preservatives. Others, such as boric acid and sodium fluoride, have specific, limited uses. Hence the choice of preservative will depend upon the agencies of deterioration (biological, mechanical etc.) against which protection is required and the conditions to which the timber will be exposed in service. In choosing a preservative, consideration should be given to the possibility that the nature or level of the hazard may change in the course of time.

1. General requirements

The biodeterioration of wood (i.e. the deterioration of wood caused by living organisms) and some forms of mechanical breakdown can be greatly reduced or retarded by the correct use of certain oils and toxic chemicals that, collectively, can be called wood preservatives. These preservatives may be applied to the green log to prevent fungal or insect damage for a few weeks before conversion; to veneer or sawn timber for short-term protection during drying, shipping or storage; or to the final product to confer resistance for many years to decay, termites, borers, marine organisms and such mechanical agencies as weathering, splitting or water absorption. Fire-retardant compounds are sometimes grouped with wood preservatives, and some proprietary products contain a mixture of fire-retardant and wood-preserving chemicals. Because of these varied uses, there are many different preservative formulations, though in general, all comply with the following main requirements.

Toxicity

The first requirement is toxicity or repellency to the organism(s) to be controlled. Few chemical compounds are equally effective against both fungi and insects, and within any group there are often some organisms that have unusual tolerance. In most cases, therefore, preservatives based on a single toxic compound are best restricted to specific uses, such as borax for lyctid and anobiid control, while mixtures are preferably used as general-purpose preservatives.

Permanence

Although a high degree of permanence is not essential for all uses, premature failure can be expected if a preservative does not withstand the conditions of service for the period required. When selecting a preservative, the conditions of service must always be considered in conjunction with the required period of service. The more volatile preservatives are unsuitable where long-term protection is required, particularly if the rate of evaporation is increased by exposure to high temperatures. Preservatives that can be leached easily from the wood are unsuitable for use under wet conditions, although they may give protection for a lifetime if the timber is kept dry.

Penetration

However toxic or permanent a preservative may be, its effectiveness over a long period is highly dependent on the type of penetration obtained in the wood. Superficial coatings or shallow or erratic penetration cannot be expected to give protection for as long as deep, uniform treatment. Such treatment is dependent on the method of application, the penetration properties of the preservative and the permeability, or treatability, of the timber. The latter is of great importance, although when sufficiently dry, the sapwood of most timbers is fairly readily penetrated. The heartwood is much more difficult to treat, and many timbers, including the eucalypts, are in the "very difficult" class. In practical terms, this means that to obtain deep, uniform penetration in sawn timber, it is necessary to select the timber species, the preservative and the treatment method with considerable care.

Other requirements

Various other properties of a preservative are either essential or desirable depending on the particular use. These include:

(a) Safety in use;

(b) Low toxicity to people;

(c) Low fire hazard;

(d) Cleanliness and absence of objectionable or persistent odour and colour;

(e) Environmental acceptability for both the treated wood and wastes;

(f) Negligible corrosive action on common metals readily identifiable or detectable in treated wood;

(g) Minimal interference with gluing, painting or other finishing;

(h) Cheapness and ready availability.

As there is no ideal preservative, it is necessary to select one that meets essential requirements and then to adjust the methods of treating and handling the timber to minimize any inherent disadvantages.

2. Classification of preservatives

There is no universally accepted system of classifying wood preservatives, but the main practical distinctions are listed in table 4.

Table 4. Types of wood preservatives

Type	Usual treatment methods	Examples of each type
Permanent oils	Pressure or open-tank (thermal process)	Creosote oils, mixtures of creosote with tar or mineral oils, oil solutions of penta-chlorophenol and creosote-pentachlorophenol mixtures
Fixed water-borne preservatives (CCA)	Pressure, sap replacement	Metal-chrome-arsenic mixtures such as Boliden, Celcure and Tanalith salts
Unfixed diffusion preservatives	Steeping, dip-diffusion, pressure-diffusion	Boron compounds, sodium fluoride and multi-salt diffusion mixtures
Aqueous dipping and spraying preservatives	Spraying or dipping to give superficial or envelope treatments	Log sprays, anti-satin dips, timber stack sprays, termite soil poisons etc.
Light organic solvent preservatives	Brushing, spraying or dipping to give superficial or envelope treatments	Water-repellent dipping preservatives, metallic naphthenates and various organic fungicides and insecticides
Glueline additives for plywood	For addition to glues used for bonding plywood	Arsenic, chlorinated hydrocarbon insecticides etc.

3. Fixed oil preservatives

Creosote oil

Creosote oil is probably the best known and most widely used preservative in the world. It is generally regarded as setting the standard of permanence and reliability for a general-purpose wood preservative for outdoor construction timbers such as railway ties, poles, marine piling etc. Almost all the creosote oil currently used in Australia for wood preservation conforms to the AS 1143-1973. It is produced by blending distillate fractions from coke-oven tar. The production closely follows the specification used in the United States for the production of high-temperature creosotes; however, owing to subtle differences in composition, the Australian creosote produces an undesirable deposit on the surface of treated wood. Transmission-line poles, when so treated, require a long period of weathering before becoming acceptable to the linesmen who must work on them. In an effort to overcome this objection, the Government and industry are working together to develop an emulsified pigmented creosote. Test results so far are promising, but additional field and laboratory testing is still necessary to confirm the preservative effectiveness of treatments made with this modified product and to ensure the acceptability of the treated timber to the workforce.

Creosote mixtures

Mixtures of creosote oil with tar or mineral oil have been used to a considerable extent in the United States, mainly for railway tie treatments. They have not been used commercially in Australia, although in experimental tests of pressure-treated radiata pine railway ties in South Australia, a 60:40 mixture of creosote and furnace oil has shown a slight superiority over creosote alone because of a small improvement in the mechanical life of the ties. This advantage, which is due to better weather protection, is common with heavy mineral oils but must be set against their tendency to form troublesome sludge when mixed with creosote.

Tar

Tar used alone is not a good wood preservative because it is less toxic than creosote and is usually less able to penetrate the wood. Its use as a surface coating to improve the service life of timber in ground contact is of doubtful value.

Pentachlorophenol and arsenic in creosote

The addition of about 2 per cent pentachlorophenol to creosote oil to increase its toxicity to fungi has gained favour in the United States for some pole treatments. It is not commercially used in Australia, but it might be useful for some round eucalypt timbers where it is difficult to obtain the desired minimum creosote retention.

The addition of arsenic trioxide to creosote to improve termite resistance is also possible and may in the future find application in areas of high termite hazard.

Pentachlorophenol in mineral oil

A 5 per cent (by weight) solution of pentachlorophenol in a non-volatile mineral oil such as furnace oil may be considered as approximately equivalent to creosote oil for the treatment of railway ties, poles etc. Compared to creosote oil, this solution has the following advantages and disadvantages:

(a) It is more resistant to weathering;

(b) It is ineffective against marine borers;

(c) It is often dirtier to handle and more likely to cause skin irritation, for which reason its use is restricted in some countries.

Although a 5 per cent solution of pentachlorophenol in heavy oil has given good results under a wide variety of conditions, it is not a good insecticide and needs to be reinforced with a persistent insecticide if required for use where there is a hazard from both decay and insects, particularly termites.

4. Fixed water-borne preservatives

Metal-chrome-arsenic salts

There have been many attempts to devise mixtures of inorganic compounds that will dissolve in water to produce stable solutions but that will react, or fix, in the wood after treatment to form more or less insoluble toxic compounds. Probably the most successful of these fixed water-borne preservatives have been the metal-chrome-arsenic salts, which are now widely used as general-purpose preservatives. As used commercially in Australia today, these are all products of the copper-chrome-arsenic (CCA) type. These preservatives should be referred to by their trade names in specifications so that equivalent retentions can be set.

Preservatives of unknown or confidential composition can rarely be recommended. The user should not be asked to trust secret formulations that may vary in composition and that cannot be assessed by a quick, practical test. The premature failure of treated wood is often disastrous but, as it may not occur for several years, it is more likely to damage the reputation of the wooden product than that of the preservative, which is easily changed in name and composition.

The composition of most of the CCA preservatives currently available commercially in Australia is listed in an appendix to AS 1604. Their elemental composition is presented in table 5.

The toxicity of these preservatives to insects is dependent almost entirely on the arsenic content, while for fungi it depends on both copper and arsenic. The chromium is relatively non-toxic, its function being mainly to control solubility and fixation and to prevent the corrosion of metals.

Differences in the toxic content of these preservatives do not indicate that one is superior to another but only that different amounts, or retentions, in the wood may be necessary to secure the same result.

The difference between oxide and salt-type formulations should be understood. In the latter, some sodium or potassium sulphate is formed as a by-product of the fixation reaction, and this may crystallize on the surface of the wood as a faint white bloom during drying of the treated timber. It is not poisonous or deleterious to the preservative and it readily washes off. In oxide formulations, this by-product is not formed. It is claimed that, for this reason, wood treated with an oxide formulation has higher practical importance even in electric transmission poles, but this is controversial.

Table 5. Elemental composition of copper-chrome-arsenic preservatives a/

| Preservative | Type of formulation | Elemental composition (%) | | | | |
		Copper	Chromium	Arsenic	Zinc	Phosphorus
Boliden K. 33	Oxide	11.8	13.8	22.3	–	–
Celcure A Celcure AP	) Salt	8.1	14.1	14.8	–	–
Tanalith C	Salt	8.9	15.9	11.3	–	–
Sarmix 3	Salt	8.9	15.9	11.3	–	–
Tanalith CA	Salt	8.9	15.5	21.0	–	–
CSIRO 3S	Salt	7.3	10.9	10.3	3.9	4.6
CSIRO 30	Oxide	10.4	15.5	14.6	5.6	6.5

a/ Some of these preservatives are now being produced with lower water content by using some anhydrous salts. However, their nominal elemental composition remains the same.

Zinc or copper pentachlorophenate

These compounds, which have low solubility in water and are very toxic to fungi, are used to a limited extent in wood preservation. Zinc pentachlorophenate has been used commercially in Australia for the treatment of plywood: the veneer is dipped into two different aqueous solutions to form the insoluble toxic compound in the wood. Copper pentachlorophenate is generally more toxic to fungi but being strongly coloured has more limited use. The addition of arsenic or other insecticides to both preservatives seems desirable where there is a termite hazard.

Other fixed preservatives

There are several other well-known preservatives that form more or less insoluble compounds in the wood. These include the following:

(a) Celcure non-arsenical: acid copper chromate;

(b) Chemonite: ammoniacal copper arsenate, ammoniacal copper caprylate, ammoniacal copper pentachlorophenate and solubilized organo-tin compounds;

(c) Wolman salts: fluor-chrome, fluor-chrome-arsenic, chrome-arsenic and copper-chrome-boron.

Some of these preservatives confer high resistance to both decay and insects and are well fixed. Others are inferior in one or another respect or have other disadvantages. All, however, are potentially usable under some conditions.

5. Non-fixed diffusion preservatives

Penetrability

With fixed water-borne preservatives such as copper-chrome-arsenic salts, which are usually applied by pressure treatment, initial penetration occurs only where the solution can be forced into the wood. Fixation within the wood is usually rapid, and these preservatives soon become insoluble and incapable of further movement. The penetration pattern is thus fairly sharply defined and any areas that resisted treatment during the pressure injection remain untreated.

Diffusion preservatives are also water-soluble but differ from fixed salts in that they do not form insoluble compounds in the wood or, at most, do so only very slowly. They thus retain their ability to move, or diffuse, in the wood over long periods if conditions are suitable. This diffusion is not a quick mass movement of solution, as occurs during pressure treatment, but is the slow passage of molecules or ions of the preservative from cell to cell through the water in the wood. Provided the wood is green or semi-green, this movement will continue in both sapwood and heartwood irrespective of whether the latter can be penetrated in pressure treatments. It will also continue in wood that has been previously dried but become wet again. Although diffusion is a relatively slow process, considerable penetration in green wood can generally be obtained from a concentrated surface application of preservative, provided the wood is prevented from drying out for a few weeks after treatment.

Application

Where more rapid treatment is required, the methods commonly used for lyctid immunization of sawn timber in Australia may be used. These are hot treatments in which the timber is either steamed or is heated in the solution and is then allowed to cool down for several hours while still immersed. Since the timber is usually either green or semi-green when treated, these methods combine an open-tank method with diffusion treatment, i.e. the volume of solution in the tank decreases because of its absorption, and its concentration also decreases because of diffusion of the preservative into the wood. As relatively weak solutions are used and as the open-tank effect is considerable, the sapwood is usually much more heavily treated than the heartwood. In lyctid immunization this is a desirable economy.

It should be clearly understood that most diffusion preservatives will leach out of wood used in ground contact or exposed to wetting for any considerable period. Diffusion preservatives are therefore suitable mainly for timber or plywood used indoors or protected from wetting by a well-maintained paint system.

As there are large differences in the rates of diffusion of different preservatives, those used in diffusion treatments should be selected as far as possible from compounds in which the toxic ions are relatively fast moving.

Diffusion preservatives

The main diffusion preservatives used or available in Australia are boron compounds, the effectiveness of which in preventing lyctid borer attack has been demonstrated for more than 30 years. These compounds have found wide use in Australia for this purpose and, more recently, in New Zealand for the prevention of both lyctid and anobiid borer damage. Also, it is now known that boron compounds have considerable toxicity to most wood-destroying fungi and useful toxicity to termites. Because of their fast diffusion rate, their low cost and the clean, colourless treatment, they are particularly suitable for diffusion treatments of building timbers.

Boron compounds

The main boron compounds of value in wood preservation are listed below. The toxic content has been expressed as per cent boron (B) in the pure compound.

Boric acid (H_3BO_3)

Boric acid (17.48% B) is usually more costly per toxic unit than borax. It also has the disadvantage that solutions used for treating wood should be kept from contact with iron. Such contact causes inky discoloration due to the formation of iron tannate. Solubility at 20° C is about 4.6 per cent m/m (4.6 g boric acid in 100 g water).

Borax decahydrate ($Na_2B_4O_7 \cdot 10H_2O$)

Because of its high water content (about 47%) and greater bulk, borax decahydrate (11.34% B) is usually less economical to use than borax pentahydrate, although otherwise it is quite suitable. Solubility at 20° C is about 4.9 per cent m/m. Unlike boric acid, it does not react with ferrous metals in a treatment plant.

Borax pentahydrate ($Na_2B_4O_7 \cdot 5H_2O$)

Borax pentahydrate (14.85% B) is widely used in Australia for the lyctid immunization of sawn timber and veneer. Because of its lower water content (about 31%) and lesser bulk than borax decahydrate, its price per toxic unit is generally lower. In common with other borate solutions for treating wood, it can be used in iron tanks without risking discoloration due to the formation of iron tannate.

Borax anhydrous ($Na_2B_4O_7$)

Borax anhydrous (21.49% B) contains no water of crystallization and is more difficult to dissolve than the hydrated forms.

Sodium 1:5 borate ($Na_2B_{10}O_{16} \cdot 10H_2O$)

Sodium 1:5 borate (18.32 B), often called sodium pentaborate, is much more soluble in cold or warm water than boric acid or borax and is hence suitable for dip-diffusion treatments where a cold or warm, concentrated solution is required. It can be purchased as pentaborate or can be made by mixing 100 parts by mass of boric acid (H_3BO_3) with 78.5 parts of borax pentahydrate ($Na_2B_4O_7 \cdot 5H_2O$). This mixture contains about 16.32 per cent B.

Sodium 1:4 borate (approximately $Na_2B_8O_{13} \cdot 4H_2O$)

Sodium 1:4 borate (20.97% B), sometimes called sodium octaborate, is highly soluble in warm water and is commonly used in dip-diffusion treatments of sawn timber in New Zealand. Up to about 20° C, it is not highly soluble, but thereafter its solubility increases more rapidly until it becomes suitable for dip-diffusion treatments requiring concentrated solutions at temperatures of 30-55° C. It can be made by mixing 100 parts by mass of boric acid (H_3BO_3) with 117.5 parts of borax pentahydrate ($Na_2B_4O_7 \cdot 5H_2O$). This mixture contains about 16.06 per cent B. Its solubility at 20° C is approximately 10 per cent m/m.

Sodium borofluorides

A highly soluble complex is formed when boric acid (H_3BO_3) and sodium fluoride (NaF) are dissolved together in the ratio of four parts by mass of H_3BO_4 to one part NaF. This mixture contains about 14 per cent B and 9 per cent F and is more soluble in cold water than the boron compounds previously described. Its solubility at 20° C is approximately 27 per cent m/m and it is particularly suitable for cold dip-diffusion treatments.

Fluorine compounds

Sodium fluoride (NaF) is used as an alternative to boron compounds for the lyctid immunization of plywood by dip-diffusion treatment of the green veneer. Unlike boron compounds, which affect the water resistance of some phenolic glues, sodium fluoride does not seem to cause any gluing problems. However, as a lycticide its cost is higher per toxic unit and more care is necessary to avoid health hazards. It is not a good termiticide.

Complex diffusion preservatives

BLUE 7 diffusion preservative

BLUE 7 diffusion preservative is particularly suitable for the in situ treatment of any partially decayed wooden member that still retains sufficient mechanical strength to be useful. Applied as a brush coating or surface spray, with slight dilution, it will penetrate damp and/or decayed wood and prevent further decay. When used in the repair of window-sills and similar building timbers, pockets of badly decayed wood should be scraped reasonably clean prior to the application of the BLUE 7.

BLUE 7 was developed for the treatment of centre rots in power poles, but it has proved to have much wider application. Recently, it has been released for general use and is now available in small lots for domestic purposes and in larger lots for industrial use. It is supplied as a concentrate consisting almost entirely of toxic components and, as supplied, contains 10.4 per cent copper, 13.1 per cent fluoride, 6.8 per cent boron and some ammonia. It is safe to handle and presents minimal pollution problems either in service, when it may be covered with paint, or in the subsequent disposal of any unwanted treated wood. The recommended rate of usage is 8-10 kg/m^3.

BLUE 7 should not be used where direct and continuous leaching is likely to occur. It is not intended for use in ground contact and, above ground, may need replenishment every five to seven years unless protected by paint.

Dip-diffusion preservative

Dip-diffusion preservative is variously known as CSIRO patent preservative, BFCA (borofluoride-chrome-arsenic) or dry-mix. Its components can be prepared in several forms, including a dry powder (hence "dry-mix"), a one-pack mix, a two-pack mix or separate components. All forms are highly soluble in cold water and will readily form solutions in excess of 30 per cent m/m concentration According to the actual formulation used, the preservative will contain 10-13 per cent elemental boron, 6-8 per cent elemental fluorine, 3-4 per cent elemental chromium and 6-8 per cent elemental arsenic.

One of the many advantages of the dip-diffusion process is that it requires no monitoring of treatment solution concentrations or composition, provided that the several components are supplied and used in their correct proportions. Immersion in the treating solution is only momentary, and contact between the green wood and the treatment solution is too brief for any differential absorption to occur. Penetration of the preservative takes place away from the treatment solution in diffusion stacks, or sweat boxes.

Dip-diffusion preservative treatment has been successfully used in Papua New Guinea for over 20 years for the control of insect attack and decay in building timbers, including exterior joinery. In spite of this satisfactory service record in tropical climates, and although some fixation may occur, this preservative is regarded as being leachable and is not recommended for use in ground contact. Best results will be obtained when it is protected from the weather by painting or when used indoors.

Aqueous dipping and spraying preservatives

Wood preservatives in this category are used mainly in superficial treatments such as the spraying of logs, anti-stain dipping or sawn timber etc., where long-term protection is usually not required. However, some are used as termite soil poisons, and in this case much higher permanence can be expected, provided the application is not superficial.

Sodium pentachlorophenate

Sodium pentachlorophenate has very high toxicity to almost all fungi including common moulds, many of which are not deterred by treatments effective against wood-destroying fungi. It is water-soluble while the solution remais alkaline but will precipitate out as the water-insoluble pentachlorophenol if the solution becomes even faintly acidic, i.e. when the pH falls below 7. For this reason, solutions used for dipping timbers often contain borax to supply an alkaline reserve, or buffer, against the acidity of the wood.

As sodium pentachlorophenate is a much better fungicide than insecticide, its use in log sprays is almost always in mixture with an insecticide intended to control borers.

Typical formulations for a log spray or an anti-stain dip for sawn timber are as follows:

	Content (%)
Log spray (% m/m)	
Sodium pentachlorophenate	2.0
Emulsifiable insecticide, such as pure lindane, dieldrin etc.	0.8
Water	97.2
Colour, if required	
Anti-stain dip or spray for sawn timber (% m/m)	
Sodium pentachlorophenate*	0.5
Borax pentahydrate ($Na_2B_4O_7 \cdot 5H_2O$)	1.5
Water	98.0

---

*Under difficult conditions, 1 per cent sodium pentachlorophenate may be necessary.

Sodium orthophenylphenate

As an alternative to sodium pentachlorophenate, sodium orthophenylphenate, which is water-soluble, is more pleasant to use and less toxic to people. In general, somewhat higher concentrations are desirable.

Sodium salicylanilide

As the toxicity to people is very low for sodium salicylanilide, which is odourless, it can be used for mould control in food stores or near foodstuffs, where most other preservatives would be objectionable.

Copper-8-quinolinate

Water-soluble formulations of copper-8-quinolinate, also called copper-8, have been tested at the New Zealand Forest Research Institute and have been shown to be suitable for application by spray or dip. Adequate control of moulds, stains and decay has been achieved with concentrations as low as 0.025 per cent active ingredient. Copper-8 is not compatible with boron salts but may be used in conjunction with emulsifiable concentrates of the chlorinated hydrocarbon insecticides. It is somewhat corrosive to iron treatment vessels, and solutions of this preservative tend to be unstable.

Emulsions and suspensions

Most modern insecticides are organic compounds that will not dissolve in water but that are widely available as emulsifiable concentrates or as water-dispersible powders. Purchased in these forms, they can be readily diluted with water to form emulsions or suspensions. Many organic fungicides can be similarly prepared if required. They have a number of uses.

Termite soil poisons

Emulsifiable concentrates of aldrin, chlordane, dieldrin, heptachlor etc. may be diluted with water and used as termite soil poisons. Some of these compounds are widely used in Australia for this purpose and if applied in accordance with the provisions of AS 2057 are effective for many years.

Timber stack sprays

These insecticides, either as emulsifiable concentrates or as wettable powders, may be used for temporary insect protection of sticks of sawn timber. Spraying with lindane or dieldrin at a concentration of 0.5 per cent m/m, calculated as pure active compound, would be a typical application. It should be noted that, with pinhole borers, this type of treatment may not prevent damage entirely in freshly sawn green timber as the beetles can drill holes for egg-laying so rapidly that some disfigurement may occur before the insecticide can take effect.

House frame timber spraying

The most persistent insecticides, both oil solutions and emulsions, have apparently been used to control powder post beetle attack in newly erected eucalypt hardwood house frames. Applied as an overall spray coating to the completed timber frame, such treatments may retard the rate at which these borers destroy susceptible sapwood, but there is no evidence that the end result is any different from what happens in houses that are not sprayed - it just takes a little longer. Such treatments are not recommended by CSIRO.

6. Light organic solvent preservatives

Light organic solvent preservatives are solutions of fungicides and insecticides either singly or in combination in non-swelling (non-aqueous) solvents. These solutions may also contain wax and resin additives intended to repel water or impede its absorption, thus contributing to the dimensional stability of the treated wood. Originally, they were intended to give short-term protection to exterior joinery during the period between delivery to a building site and completion of the structure. In more recent times, there has been a tendency to expect longer-term protection from them.

Penetration

These preservatives were once mainly applied by spraying, brushing or short-term dipping, but more recently they have been increasingly used in vacuum/pressure systems. With most timbers, the penetration obtained with surface application or short-term dipping is only superficial and, on the side grain, the protective envelope may be very thin indeed. End-grain penetration is usually deeper but varies greatly with the timber species and with the presence of sapwood. With relatively impermeable timbers, such as eucalypt heartwood, the end-grain penetration obtained from a three-minute dip may amount to only a few millimetres, while with absorbent timbers or sapwood, it may exceed 250 mm. With the modern vacuum/pressure cycles sometimes used, penetration depends on both the treatment schedule and the permeability of the wood. In any case, and for best results, light organic solvent preservatives should be applied only to seasoned wood after all machining and fitting has been completed.

Application

As a general rule, superficial treatments do not give effective protection to timber used in ground contact or fully exposed to the weather. Their main use is for timbers in service above-ground, where the hazard is moderate and intermittent and where they are given some additional protection by painting or are otherwise sheltered, as by a roof overhang. Typically, they are used to protect exterior joinery by inhibiting water absorption at the joints and by serving as a protective envelope against decay and insect attack. When timber so treated is cut or machined after treatment, the freshly exposed surfaces should be given a saturating application of the preservative solution to restore the protective envelope.

Light organic solvent preservatives are now being offered for many purposes for which they were not originally intended. Some of these uses may involve high hazards, or even soil contact. Under such conditions of exposure, they cannot be expected to give as much protection as conventional pressure impregnation treatments with fixed preservatives or with creosote oil and other preservatives in a heavy, non-volatile oil.

Components

Copper naphthenate

A solution of copper naphthenate in mineral turpentine or white spirits, containing at least 2 per cent metallic copper, has been used as a coating or dipping preservative for many years. It is durable, has a reasonable measure of water repellency and is quite effective against both decay and insects. It has also been used, prior to painting, on wooden boats, inside for protection against decay and outside for protection against marine borers. After the solvent has evaporated, it has low toxicity to green plants, so it can be used for the treatment of seed boxes.

Copper naphthenate has a persistent and rather unpleasant odour and is usually slow to dry, but if allowed to dry for long enough, it can be painted over. It has a strong, persistent green colour.

Pentachlorophenol

Pentachlorophenol is very toxic to fungi, but it is not particularly effective against insects. When used in modern, general-purpose preservative formulations, it is usually reinforced by the addition of a persistent insecticide such as aldrin, chlordane, dieldrin or heptachlor. It may also be fortified with tributyl tin oxide in some of the formulations used in vacuum/pressure treatment of joinery etc. The formulations may also contain timber-stabilizing and water-repellent compounds. If treated timber is cut, the protective envelope should be restored by saturating the freshly exposed surfaces with preservative.

Pentachlorophenol is toxic to people and is liable to cause dermatitis. It has been banned in some countries. In spite of its disadvantages, it has been widely used and will no doubt continue to be used for some time but with considerably more care and attention to sensible precautions.

Tributyl tin oxide

Tributyl tin oxide is the principal toxicant in many solvent-based preservatives, particularly in those used for the vacuum/pressure impregnation of exterior joinery. Although it has insecticidal properties, most proprietary formulations contain insecticides as well as resins and waxes. Tributyl tin oxide is particularly effective against brown rots and, used in conjunction with other fungicides such as pentachlorophenol or quaternary ammonium compounds, it can be a very effective preservative.

7. Glueline additives

Borer and termite attack on plywood can be controlled effectively by the addition of suitable insecticides to the glue. This simple treatment can be used with most glues but has special application to phenolic resins used for exterior and marine-grade plywoods. With these grades of plywood, neither boron compounds nor sodium fluoride, both of which are readily leachable, can be recommended for a product that is sold as waterproof. Insecticides that are not readily leached and that give good control of borers and termites when incorporated into the glue are, therefore, attractive. The recommended glueline additives are amply described and provided for in AS 1604.

So far, the addition of preservatives to the glueline has not been accepted by Australian research workers as a suitable means of increasing the decay resistance of plywood.

E. Extending the service life of timber (timber preservation)

Introduction

Having chosen a preservative suitable to the anticipated hazard and service condition, the quantity, or retention, of the preservative and its distribution, or penetration, into the wood can be greatly affected by the treatment process. The choice of process will depend upon many factors, including the condition of the wood at the time of treatment, e.g. its moisture content; the timber species (some species are more permeable than others); whether the sections to be treated are natural rounds or sawn (sapwood is always more permeable than heartwood of the same species); the hazard and degree of exposure to which the treated timber will be subjected in service (e.g. building timber protected from the weather is generally at lower risk than exterior joinery, and timber used in ground contact is at higher risk than timber used underground).

A wide range of treatment processes is available to the modern practitioner of wood preservation. These range from simple surface applications and diffusion treatments requiring little capital expenditure to sophisticated commercial operations using high autoclaves (or cylinders) with automatic control of treatment variables such as vacuum and pressure, time and temperature, coupled to capacious storage tanks and backed up by modern laboratory facilities for quality assurance. In commercial ventures, the scale of the operation will be related to the capitalization of the treatment plant.

AS 1604 attempts to equate preservative penetration and retentions to the natural durability of the heartwood of the treated wood and the severity of the hazard to which it is likely to be exposed in service. It also lists the major commercial preservatives available in Australia. It does not place any restriction on the treatment process but indicates results to be attained.

1. Pressure treatment

When pressure is applied to the liquid in which permeable timber is immersed, the rate and depth of penetration are increased. This is the basis of all pressure treatment. Vacuum/pressure is a term used to cover most forms of such commercial treatments, because they employ a vacuum in the treatment cycles.

The first requirement for the process is a steel pressure vessel or autoclave with a pressure-tight door. The door can be held by bolts, but quick-locking doors with hydraulic seals have obvious advantages.

The basic plant, shown in figure 3, requires a working tank with a contents gauge; a pressure pump for applying pressure to the liquid in the pressure cylinder; a vacuum pump to fill it and to remove surplus preservative from the surface of the timber; and the necessary ancilliary piping and valves. In addition, a circulating pump may be provided for pumping preservative between the cylinder and the tank or for mixing by recirculation.

Figure 3. Basic pressure treatment plant design

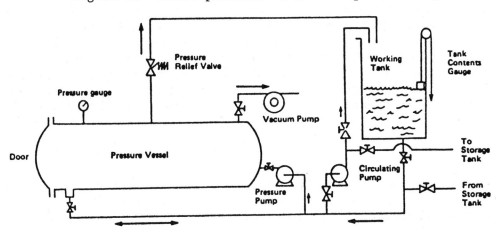

The pressure cylinder must be protected by safety valves. A gauge for pressure or vacuum/pressure is essential. Plants using heat have a pressure/temperature recorder on the cylinder and a thermometer on the working tank. A storage tank for reserve supplies is necessary in a plant using oil, and a mixing tank with mechanical stirrer or other means of agitation is necessary in a plant using water-borne salts. Pressure vessels are usually required to withstand vacuum and hydraulic pressure of 140 kPa (gauge) for low-pressure treatment and up to 7,000 kPa (gauge) for high-pressure treatment.

To facilitate manipulation, some types of preservative require heating to reduce viscosity before they are pumped into the pressure cylinder. This is usually accomplished by heating with steam coils or by employing a heat exchanger, although in small plants electrical heaters can be used. When heat is applied, both the cylinder and the tank must be adequately insulated.

Cylinders vary in size from 1.8 m long x 1 m in diameter (for the treatment of fence posts) to more than 25 m long (for poles). Some cylinders are made large enough to accept packs of sawn timber already stripped for drying to avoid the extra handling costs, but such large cylinders require much more liquid to fill them and it is sometimes cheaper to treat more charges in a smaller cylinder, in spite of the extra handling costs.

Timber is loaded on steel bogies, which run into the cylinder on rails over a movable bridge that is removed to operate the door. These rails can connect with tracks to other parts of the plant. Light timbers must be restrained and the bogies held down to prevent them floating off the rails when the cylinder is flooded.

2. Types of pressure treatment

Different sequences of cycles of vacuum, air pressure and liquid pressure are used to obtain treatment retentions with various timbers and preservatives. There are different treatments for different purposes.

Full-cell treatment (Bethell process)

As its name implies, full-cell treatment leaves the cells in permeable timber full of liquid. Vacuum is first applied to the cylinder to remove as much air as possible from the timber (figure 4). The same vacuum is maintained while the cylinder is filled with preservative solution and pressure is then applied until refusal* is reached. The pressure is related and the cylinder emptied, after which a short final vacuum is applied to recover "drip" or waste that would otherwise occur; finally the vacuum is released.

Commonly, a 2-3 hr treatment, including initial and final vacuums of 30 min each, is required for a permeable timber such as Pinus radiata sapwood. Much longer vacuum and pressure periods may be needed with semi-permeable timbers, such as the heartwood of Western hemlock, Tsuga heterophylla, to obtain sufficient retention and penetration of the preservative. Total treatment times of 12 hr or even longer are costly but may be inexpensive when compared with the cost of a premature failure in service of imperfectly treated material.

---

*Refusal is defined as the stage in the treatment when the quantity of preservative absorbed in any two consecutive 15 min periods does not exceed 1 per cent of the amount already absorbed.

Figure 4. Full-cell treatment (Bethell)

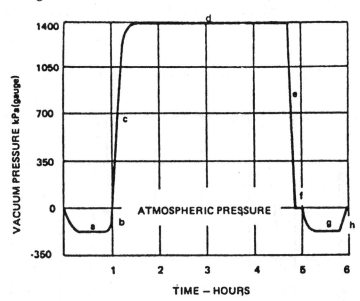

a Preliminary Vacuum Period
b Fill Cylinder with Preservative
c Build up Pressure
d Maximum Pressure Held

e Release Pressure
f Empty Cylinder of Preservative
g Final Vacuum Period
h Release Vacuum

Full-cell treatment is also used for the treatment of semi-permeable or refractory heartwood with preservative oils. Hardwood railway ties are usually treated in this way to obtain maximum retentions.

Empty-cell treatments

These treatments depend on the expansion of air trapped in the timber during treatment to expel excess preservative from the cells after pressure has been released. Their use is essential when maximum penetration without excessive retention of preservative oils is required in more permeable timbers.

Lowry process

The Lowry process (figure 5) is the simplest and most commonly used form of empty-cell treatment. The preservative is admitted to the cylinder without drawing an initial vacuum, and atmospheric air is released from the top of the cylinder as it fills with liquid. When pressure is applied, the air in the timber is compressed as the liquid is forced into the timber. After the desired gross absorption of liquid has been achieved, preferably at refusal, the pressure is released and a short final vacuum is applied during which time a proportion of the liquid, known as the kick-back, is forced out by expansion of the air compressed in the cell cavities.

Rueping process

In the Rueping process (figure 6), the charge is sealed in the cylinder, which is then filled with compressed air to a predetermined pressure. Preservative is then pumped in against this pressure, which is prevented from rising by bleeding air from the top of the cylinder as the cylinder fills. When the cylinder is full hydraulic pressure is applied followed by a final vacuum. Kick-back is greater with this process than with the Lowry cycle and it is mainly used for every permeable lightweight timbers. In Australia it has been used for treating radiata pine with creosote for poles, posts and railway ties, where control of final retention is essential for economy and to prevent bleeding.

Figure 5.   Lowry empty–cell treatment

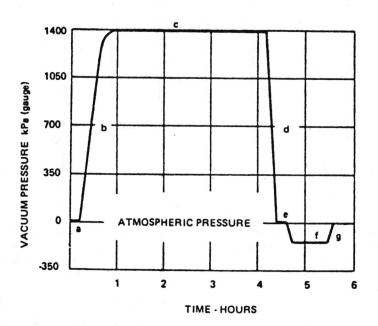

a Fill Cylinder with Preservative at Atmospheric Pressure
b Build up Pressure
c Maximum Pressure Held
d Release Pressure

e Empty Cylinder of Preservative
f Final Vacuum Period
g Release Vacuum

Figure 6.   Rueping empty–cell treatment

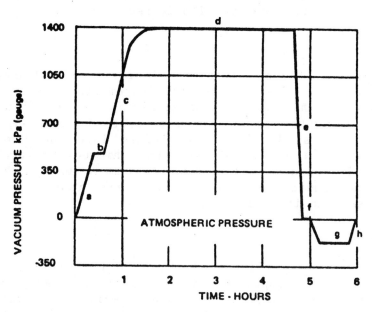

a Preliminary Air Pressure Applied
b Fill Cylinder hold Air Pressure
c Build up Pressure
d Maximum Pressure Held

e Release Pressure
f Empty Cylinder of Preservative
g Final Vacuum Period
h Release Vacuum

Oscillating pressure process

The oscillating pressure method (figure 7) is a variation of the full-cell process for the treatment of softwoods of high moisture content with water-borne preservatives. By the use of rapidly alternating cycles of vacuum and hydraulic pressure, it replaces some of the free water, or sap, in the timber with preservative solution. An automatic controller is used to apply vacuum pressure cycles to the pressure cylinder.

Figure 7. Oscillating-pressure treatment

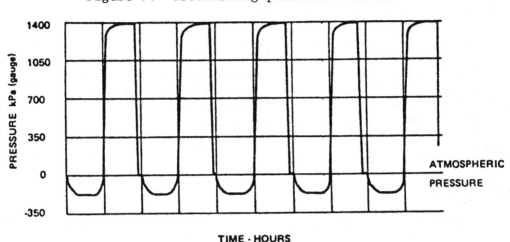

Research in New Zealand has shown that _Pinus radiata_ can be successfully treated by this method provided that it is partly air-dried first and that the repeated application and release of pressure is sufficient without the use of vacuum. The process in use in New Zealand uses boron compounds as the preservative. With CCA preservatives, the process requires careful control of solution strength and chemical balance as these may alter during treatment.

Double vacuum

This process depends primarily on creating a vacuum inside the timber and then using this to draw preservative fluid into the timber. The impregnation period is usually at atmospheric pressure, although in some variations it may still be under vacuum. With semi-permeable timbers, or to obtain high preservative loading, a positive pressure may also be used when it is necessary.

A final vacuum serves to remove excess preservative from within the wood. The complete penetration of permeable sapwood is achieved, but retentions are controlled at a low level since the double vacuum technique is used with organic solvent preservatives to treat window-frames and other building timbers that are to be painted.

Liquified gas process

This process utilizes a gas such as butane, which can be liquified by cooling or by compression and used as a solvent for organic preservatives. The treatment is a pressure process in which nearly all the excess solvent evaporates from the wood at the conclusion of the treatment cycle; it renders the wood ready for immediate use.

The wood is placed in a treatment cylinder and an initial vacuum is applied. The cylinder is then purged with an inert gas until safe conditions have been achieved and a second vacuum is applied. The preservative solution is then run into the cylinder and the pressure is increased by applying heat. At the conclusion of the pressure phase, excess liquid is returned to storage and the pressure in the treatment cylinder slowly reduced down to vacuum conditions. A second inert gas purge is then applied, and when safe conditions have been achieved the wood may be removed from the cylinder.

The process possesses the advantage that penetration of some semi-permeable species can be achieved and the wood is immediately ready for finishing because there is no solvent.

3. Non-pressure treatment

Although pressure treatment is generally regarded as the basis of commercial preservation, the methods described below are important for particular purposes and in some instances are the only means of treating a particular type of timber or of treating timber in situ.

Surface treatments

Surface coatings

Brushing

Brushing, the simplest and most readily available method of applying a wood preservative, is particularly suited for use by the general public and for on-site treatments in buildings, particularly where the working of pre-treated timber exposes a fresh surface. It is mostly associated with organic solvent wood preservatives or with lower viscosity grades of creosote.

Preservatives should be brushed on to clean and dry timber in flood coats, with the second and any subsequent coats being applied after the previous coat has soaked in but before it has dried. The preservative should not be brushed out to cover a large area; instead, sufficient flood application must be given to achieve the application rate recommended for the preservative being used. This usually necessitates two or three applications.

The preservative should be applied at the appropriate rate to all sides of the wood and must be flooded on to the end grain. When treating made-up components, e.g. furniture, the preservative should be flooded into joints. When used for woodworm eradication, it is beneficial to flood it into old flight holes.

The life of superstructures such as fencing and huts and sheds will be extended by several years by the brush application of a suitable preservative and may be prolonged almost indefinitely by applications of wood preservative at intervals of three or four years. Care must be taken to ensure the preservative enters all the joints where water might lodge.

Spraying

The spray application of wood preservatives is generally comparable in its results to brush application and can be carried out as an alternative to brush treatment under appropriate circumstances. Spray treatment is the most common method of applying wood preservatives in the in situ eradication of woodworm.

The preservative should be flooded on to the surface until a slight run-off occurs. If the resultant absorption is less than that recommended for the preservative being used, further applications should be made after the initial treatment has soaked in but before it has dried.

For pre-treatment, the preservative should be applied to all sides of the timber, and for in situ eradication, to all accessible sides. Particular regard should be paid to end grain and joints, which should be thoroughly flooded.

Deluging

In deluging, the timber is passed through an enclosed tunnel in which preservative is applied to it from various types of jet. In different makes of deluge tunnels, these vary from spray jets similar to those used in normal spray applications to a number of small jets or a single jet from a large-diameter pipe.

Deluging is mostly used for application of organic solvent preservatives, but tar oils, creosote and certain types of water-borne preservatives may also be applied by this method.

Because they offer greater throughput and more uniform application, deluge treatments can be used for the pre-treatment of timber in industrial situations where a brush or spray treatment might also be considered.

Bandage applications

Bandage treatments are useful in prolonging the life of poles that are partly decayed. A porous medium or an emulsion containing a diffusable preservative is applied to the surface of the pole at the ground-line. Diffusion of the preservative outwards into the soil at, and below, the ground-line is prevented by a waterproof membrane.

CSIRO has developed a bandage system in which polyurethane foam has been pre-impregnated with diffusable fungitoxic chemicals contained within an outer protective sheath of polyethylene. The bandage is applied to the pole at the ground-line and is heat-shrunk into place to ensure a close fit.

Oxy-char process

This process is an effective maintenance treatment used on standing, de-sapped, durable poles showing partial decay. Checks and decay pockets at the ground-line are scraped free of soil and scoured with a very hot flame, which burns all the decayed wood and sterilizes the wood adjacent to it. The surface of the pole is then charred and, while still hot, is sprayed with creosote. The disadvantage of the treatment is the small loss of cross-section that occurs each time it is repeated, usually every three to six years.

Cold soaking

The effectiveness of this treatment is related to the time for which the timber is immersed. With many of the preservatives prepared for these treatments, the recommended immersion times range from three minutes (dip treatment) for many building timbers to several hours for fence posts in ground contact or other hazardous situations.

The clean and dry timbers are totally immersed in a tank of preservative fluid. Immersion treatment is used for all types of wood preservatives, but it is most usual with organic solvent preservatives or low-viscosity creosote. The treatment is normally carried out in ambient temperatures.

An exception to total immersion is the butt treatment of fence and other posts, where an effective, economical treatment can be given by soaking the butt end only, to about 300 mm above ground level, in preservative for several hours and treating the remainder by a much shorter immersion or by brush or spray.

Hot and cold bath process

This process involves heating the dry timber in steam, hot water or liquid preservative to drive out most of the air, followed by cooling in preservative, when the atmospheric pressure assists capillary forces in moving the liquid to replace the air driven out. Heating is best done close to the boiling point (100° C) or higher if oil or steam are used. The heating time is approximately proportional to the thickness. As a general rule, one hour at the maximum temperature is required for each 25 mm of thickness, but where poles or round timbers require treatment of a narrow sapwood only, this time may be reduced. Where time is not critical, e.g. in an overnight treatment, it may be expedient to reheat the preservative the next day to drive off surplus liquid and improve surface cleanliness. This is known as an expansion bath.

Hot and cold bath treatment can be done very simply in a drum over an open fire, but for effective control and safety the preservative is usually heated by steam coils or low-temperature electric elements in an insulated tank. Poles and posts can be treated full length in the horizontal position or butt-treated in the vertical position to save heat and preservative where protection of the sapwood above ground is not essential. In either case, adequate lifting gear is needed. Hot and cold bath treatment is not used with the "fixed" CCA preservatives, solutions of which are not stable at high temperatures. It is a very satisfactory method of treatment with creosote and other oily preservatives or with solutions of single water-borne salts.

Sapwood replacement methods

This term covers a variety of similar treatments of green round timber in which some of the free water or sap is removed from the sapwood and replaced by a water-borne preservative solution. One method, the Boucherie process, in which a solution under pressure is applied to one end of the freshly cut log or pole, has been in use in Europe for over a hundred years. Modern variations of this include the application of a vacuum to one end of the log or even immersing the log in liquid under pressure at the same time.

A simple form of sap replacement can be used to treat round hardwood fence posts and small poles. Freshly cut green posts are barked and their butts immersed in a 3.5 per cent solution of copper-chrome-arsenic. As the sap evaporates from the exposed surfaces, solution is drawn up to replace it. Before all the solution is used, the posts are inverted to treat the top ends. In good drying weather, posts can be treated in about one week. Although the distribution of preservative in the sapwood is not uniform, the treatment has proved both cheap and effective. In remote areas where impregnation facilities are lacking, this process is very cheap and simple for people wanting a few posts for their own use.

The sap replacement process is recommended for treating sound, green hardwood posts with water-borne preservatives. The hot and cold bath method is used to treat dry timber with oils and oily preservatives, e.g. creosote. CSIRO experimentally treated some Victorian green pine posts using a variation of this process. Freshly cut posts were substantially, but not completely, immersed (vertically or inclined) in hot creosote for about six hours at 90-100° C and were then allowed to cool to 50° C, usually overnight. A very thorough treatment of the softwood posts resulted.

Diffusion processes

These processes are based on the fact that chemicals in solution will move from zones of high concentration into zones of low concentration through a permeable material such as wood. This principle operates when treating green timber with chemical preservatives in aqueous solution. The molecules or ions of the dissolved preservative move from the zone of high concentration in the solution to the zone of lower concentration in the wood.

The rate of movement of chemicals into wet wood is governed by factors such as the density of the timber, solution concentration and temperture. It has been established as follows:

(a) The concentration of preservative at a given depth in the timber after a given time is proportional to the solution concentration;

(b) The depth of penetration of a required concentration is directly proprotional to the square root of the time of immersion for any solution concentration;

(c) The rate of diffusion is approximately doubled for each 20° C rise in temperature.

These relationships are used to determine approximate treatment schedules with different forms of diffusion treatment, but because of variation between and within species they must be checked by frequent chemical analyses.

Simple diffusion

Simple diffusion involves water-soluble single salts dissolved in water. Green timber is immersed in the solution for hours or days, depending on species, size, concentration and temperature of the solution, to allow sufficient salt to move into the timber. This process is principally used for the immunization of sapwood. The preservative in the wood is not fixed and will leach out.

Dip-diffusion

Dip-diffusion was developed by CSIRO. After sawing, the green timber is immersed in a strong solution of a multi-salt diffusion preservative, e.g. a patented combination of boron, fluorine, chromium and arsenic compounds. After momentary immersion, the timber is then close-piled under cover to restrict drying for several weeks while the preservative diffuses into the wood. The process is widely used in Papua New Guinea for the treatment of building timbers of mixed species.

Timber treated by the above two processes is unsuitable for use under wet conditions such as ground contact or for external use unless protected by paint, as the preservative salts remain water-soluble.

Double diffusion

The purpose of the double-diffusion method is to form a preservative salt that is resistant to leaching within the wood, by reaction between suitable chemicals. This can be accomplished, for example, by first soaking green posts in a solution of copper sulphate long enough for sufficient chemical to diffuse into the wood and by then immersing them in a second solution containing sodium chromate with or without sodium arsenate. As the second solution diffuses into the wood, a precipitate is formed that is toxic to fungi and very resistant to leaching. The solution concentrations must be carefully checked before each treatment to ensure satisfactory fixation of the chemicals. Full-length treatment by this procedure has given excellent results with fence posts, and the method is also used for the _in situ_ treatment of the wood in water cooling towers, usually by spraying the first solution onto the wood and, after a suitable interval, spraying the second solution.

4. Factors affecting preservative treatment

Inherent factors

Timber species

While some treatment plants deal with only one species, such as _Pinus radiata_, most treat a variety of timbers. Plants treating sawn timber will have very mixed results if impermeable timber is included in lots of treatment. The proper identification and segregation of species is essential if consistently satisfactory treatments are to be obtained.

Problems can occur at commercial pressure plants that treat eucalypt poles if the species are not properly identified by the pole cutter. Many species are difficult to tell apart after they have been barked, so there is always a risk of including refractory species in a charge of mixed species.

Density

Density is an important factor in determining the depth of penetration and amount of liquid preservative that any timber will absorb. In general, lighter timbers can be penetrated more readily and absorb more liquid than denser ones, but for anatomical and structural reasons there are many exceptions to this rule, for example, Douglas fir, Baltic spruce and balsa. Pit aspiration and blockage of vessels in heartwood by xyloses are typical anatomical factors that can affect penetration.

The user or timber treater must be aware of the maximum preservative retention that can be obtained in a timber of any given density. Knowing that, he or she can decide what type of treatment and what concentration of solution to use.

Factors that can be controlled or modified

Moisture content

The most important factor, after inherent treatability, that affects preservative penetration and retention is moisture content. Many techniques, mainly non-pressure processes, are being developed to treat timber with water-borne and oil preservatives at moisture contents above the fibre saturation point (25-30 per cent). The general practice in Australia is to dry all treatable timber to a point below this figure for pressure treatment.

Retention and penetration are further improved in the sapwood of eucalypt poles if these are fully dried to equilibrium moisture content (12-15 per cent in southern Australia) before treatment.

Timber can be dried in the treatment cylinder by boultonizing, which consists of boiling under vacuum in creosote or preservative oil before applying a pressure treatment process. The technique is well established in Australia as a commercial treatment for hardwood railway ties.

Prefabrication

As a general rule it is desirable that all machining of timber be done before it is treated. This is particularly important with refractory timbers, in which end-grain penetration is usually all that is obtained. In fact, most prefabrication or machining is done before treatment because it is more convenient. For example, railway ties are adzed and bored, poles are machined for cross-arms and caps, bolt holes are drilled, cross-arms are bored for bolts and insulation pins, and timber for log cabins and cooling tower components is fully machined.

Incising is a form of prefabrication specifically designed to improve penetration, particularly into refractory heartwood through side-grain surfaces. Machines for this purpose make a regular pattern of incisions with sharp knives at intervals of about 50 mm along the grain and 25 mm across it, usually to a depth of 18 mm. Incising is used overseas on railway ties and poles of refractory timbers such as Douglas fir and, in Australia, for the impregnation of eucalypt railway ties with creosote or oily preservatives. Incising may also give more uniform drying when done on green material, thus reducing the risk of splitting.

Bark must be removed as it will retard drying and, in softwoods, will prevent radial penetration. Any bark is a nuisance in a treatment plant, where it can come loose and obstruct valves or strainers.

5. Preservative penetration and retention

No matter how good the preservative, a treatment will not be effective unless the retention, or amount of preservative present in the treated wood, is sufficient to repel or destroy the invading organisms and unless the penetration, or distribution of preservative in the treated wood, is such that no improperly treated wood is accessible to invading organisms.

Usually, shallow penetrations are indicative of low retentions, and deep penetration will result in high retentions. However, when retentions are expressed in terms of volumes of treated wood, as opposed to total volume of wood treated, preservative retention need not be related to the depth of penetration.

Current Australian standards and specifications tend to require treated timbers to satisfy penetration requirements before being tested for compliance with retention requirements. Fortunately, with most preservatives, penetration is more readily determined than is retention.

Penetration

Penetration is usually checked by boring treated wood at the conclusion of the treatment. With poles and other round timber, an increment borer (hollow-core borer) is commonly used to extract a radial plug from the side of the pole or post, usually at about mid-length. Such a plug or core can be split and penetration can be accurately measured and, if necessary, retained for reference.

With water-borne preservatives, the colour of the treated wood may be indicative of preservative penetration, but most commercial operators rely on specific chemical indicators. For example, turmeric is used to detect boron compounds, while chrome-asural S and rubeanic acid are indicators for CCA-type preservatives.

With creosote and other oily preservatives, chilling the plug before splitting will retard the "bleeding" (creeping or smearing) of the oil and so allow more time for an accurate measurement.

Retention

According to the type of commodity being treated, preservative retentions will be based on average or charge* retentions or on the retention or preservative in individual pieces. Furthermore, a distinction must be made between retentions expressed in terms of total volume and those referring only to treated wood volume.

For example, with fence posts of P. radiata, which has a wide, permeable sapwood, practically the whole of the post will be treatable and there will be little difference between treated volume and total volume. With eucalypt hardwood posts, only a narrow, outer annulus of sapwood will be treatable and the treated volume is likely to be much less than one third of the total volume.

Water-borne preservative salt retentions are expressed as either (a) the amount of active ingredient as a percentage of the oven-dry weight of the wood or (b) the net dry salt retention, which is measured in kg dry salt/m^3.

With these preservatives, the solution concentration can be varied to control uptake: a small volume of concentrated solution delivers as much chemical as a larger volume of a dilute solution.

The retention of creosote and oil-borne preservatives is generally expressed as total preservative uptake, e.g. kg/m^3 of 5 per cent solution of preservative in oil.

Retentions determined from charge volumes apply to the charge as a whole. Where the variation, or scatter, of retentions between pieces in a charge is required, individual retentions can be found by weighing the pieces before and after treatment. Samples of, for instance, borings taken from individual pieces can be analysed by chemical or other means, but because of the variations in loading that can occur within the piece itself, this method does not necessarily give the same result. However, it is usually all that is practicable.

In the case of round timbers with a relatively narrow band of treatable sapwood, such as the eucalypts, the volume of treatable timber in a charge must be estimated, before treatment, from measurements of mean girth and mean sapwood thickness for each pole. This, in turn, depends on a clear definition of the sapwood-heartwood boundary, which often requires the use of a chemical

----

*One charge is a single load of timber in a pressure cylinder.

indicator. Dimethyl yellow in alcohol and water is effective with many eucalypts.

Accurate determination of the average charge retention requires the following:

(a) Measurement of the volume of liquid preservative used, from the difference between the initial and final tank gauge readings, with proper allowance for drip, leads and evaporation and corrections for changes in volume due to changes in temperature;

(b) Determination of the volume of timber treated. With round timbers, this may be calculated from the girth, length and sapwood thickness of the individual rounds, but penetration should be checked against sapwood thickness for a representative sample;

(c) Checking the concentration of salt in aqueous preservatives by chemical analysis or by measurement of specific gravity. Water-borne preservatives can vary in concentration as a result of imperfect mixing, precipitation or selective absorption by the timber of individual components from a mixture.

The determination of preservative retention is unreliable with those treatment processes in which green wood is used and where the timber can lose water during treatment. This applies to certain types of diffusion treatment and to processes where green (unseasoned) timber is strongly heated.

6. After-treatment

Removal of timber from the treatment plant does not necessarily complete the treatment process. Oil treatments may require a period of air-drying to make the timber clean enough to handle. Heavy petroleum oils and coal tar rarely dry out completely and are therefore reserved for purposes such as railway ties and marine piling, where resistance to weathering or leaching is more important than a clean surface. Creosote and the lighter oils require different drying times depending on the timber, the retention and weather conditions.

With appropriate protective clothing, timber impregnated with water-borne preservative may be handled soon after treatment. However, if it is to be used for mouldings or for any other purpose where properly dried timber is essential, surface drying is not enough, and the cost of complete re-drying must be allowed for.

In spite of their poisonous nature, preservative oils and water-borne preservatives are generally safe to handle if normal precautions are observed. Most preservative oils have irritant properties with distinctive odours, which combine to ensure that they are handled carefully. Copper-chrome-arsenic preservatives, once impregnated into the timber, are insoluble, which minimizes the hazard to health. Skin irritations can occur when plant operators handle either type of preservative, but they are more likely if handlers are careless about washing or wearing gloves and aprons.

The disposal of waste from treatment plants requires some care. Creosote and preservative oils will contaminate streams so that plant effluent should have some form of trap to retain as much as possible. CCA water-borne preservatives are toxic in solution and should never be released into streams. Discharges are subject to strict environmental controls.

Small quantities of waste timber treated with CCA preservatives may be burnt in an open space but should never be used for cooking or in a barbecue. The remaining ash will contain some soluble arsenic and should be buried in a safe place away from streams and ground water. It has been found to kill garden plants.

7. Quality control of treated timber

At the present time, no single authority is responsible for specifying or maintaining standards of preservative treatment in Australia. The forest departments of Queensland and New South Wales control preservative treatment by state legislation. In Victoria, the Forests Commission has been given similar authority but does not exercise it. The Standards Association of Australia has produced standard specifications covering items such as preservative-treated transmission poles and building timbers. Various electricity supply authorities and Telecom Australia have their own specifications for treated poles and cross-arms and maintain their own inspection services at treatment plants. The Timber Preservers' Association of Australia is concerned with maintaining high standards of treatment within the industry.

Defective treatments of timber may be caused by one or a combination of the following factors: insufficient drying; poor plant control; poor quality and incorrect concentration of preservatives; insufficient treatment time, pressure or temperature; treating mixed charges; incorrect processes etc. When faulty treatment is detected, its cause should be traced and eliminated with the help of preservative suppliers, state forest departments and other authorities.

Large items such as transmission poles are usually labelled with information such as the timber species, the treater's name and the date of treatment. Sawn timber and plywood can only be identified as treated by branding or colour coding each piece. Despite some objections to the extra cost and complications in production, branding must eventually be accepted. Without it, there is considerable risk that untreated timber may be sold as treated or that timber treated for a low exposure rating may be sold or used for situations where much more severe hazards exist. In New Zealand this risk has been recognized, and all treated timber is required to be branded and colourless preservatives identified by a dye. The branding of immunized timber is required by law in Queensland and New South Wales.

8. Plywood, particle board and hardboard preservation

While the same processes can be used to treat plywood as are used to treat solid timber, there are some important differences. Unless plywood is specifically made wholly of sapwood or permeable heartwood veneers, it cannot be effectively pressure-treated in made-up form if complete penetration is required. Also, the re-drying of plywood pressure-treated with water-borne preservatives becomes increasingly difficult as the thickness increases.

In spite of this, large quantities of waterproof plywood, pre-cut to finished size, are treated with high loadings of CCA salts for use in cooling towers, where it is proving very satisfactory and re-drying is not needed. The simplest way to preserve plywood is by pre-treating the veneers. This can be done by dip-diffusion of green veneers and pressure treatment of dry veneers.

A large proportion of Australian plywood production is already immunized against lyctid attack, usually by the momentary dip-diffusion treatment of veneers, but some is immunized by adding insecticide to the glueline. The latter method is very effective against termites and offers some possibilities for protection against decay when thin veneers are used.

Reconstituted boards can be treated by adding preservatives or insecticides during manufacture or in special cases by soaking the finished board in preservative oils. Treatment is rarely specified, but some hardboards are treated to prevent termite attack.

References

1. "Water sprays prevent losses in softwood log dumps", Forest Products Newsletter, No. 304, 1964.

2. Ratcliffe, Gay and Greaves, Australian Termites (Melbourne, CSIRO, 1952).

Bibliography

CSIRO, Division of Building Research, Prevention and control of termite attack. Information sheet 10-66. Melbourne, 1966.

_____ Porotermes adamsoni (Frogatt) - a dampwood termite. Information sheet 10-69. Melbourne, 1969.

_____ The troublesome termite (white ant). Information sheet 10-71. Melbourne, 1971.

Hadlngton, P. and N. G. Cooney. A guide to pest control in Australia. Sydney, New South Wales University Press, 1974.

Hickin, N. E. Termites - a world problem. London, Rentokil Library, 1971.

Hunt and Garratt. Wood preservation. New York, McGraw-Hill, 1953.

Nicholas, D. D. Wood deterioration and its prevention by preservative treatments. New York, Syracuse University Press, 1973. 2 v.

Richardson, B. A. Wood preservation. London, Construction Press, 1978.

Standards Association of Australia. Australian Standard K55-1964; creosote oil for the preservation of timber. Sydney, 1964.

_____ Australian Standard 1143-1973; high temperature creosote oil for the preservation of timber. Sydney, 1973.

_____ Australian Standard 1144-1973; arsenical creosote for the preservation of timber. Sydney, 1973.

_____ Australian Standard 1604-1974; preservative-treated sawn timber, veneer and plywood. Sydney, 1974.

_____ Australian Standard 1605-1974; sampling and analysis of wood preservatives and preservatives-treated wood. Sydney, 1974.

_____ Australian Standard 1606- and 1607-1974; water-repellent treatment of timber and joinery. Sydney, 1974.

_____ Australian Standard 1608-1974; preservative-treated farm fencing timber. Sydney, 1974.

_____ Australian Standard 1694-1974; physical barriers used in the protection of buildings against subterranean termites. Sydney, 1974.

_____ Australian Standard 2057-1977; soil treatment for the protection of buildings against subterranean termites. Sydney, 1977.

_____ Australian Standard 2178-1978; the treatment of subterranean termite infestation in existing buildings. Sydney, 1978.

_____ Australian Standard 2209-1979; timber poles for overhead lines. Sydney, 1979.

United States Department of Agriculture. Wood handbook. Agriculture handbook No. 72. Washington, D.C., United States Government Printing Office, 1955.

Walters, N. E. Australian house fungi. Forest products technical note No. 13. Melbourne, CSIRO, Division of Building Research, 1973.

Wilkinson, J. G. Industrial timber preservation. London, Associated Business Press, 1979.

II. FIRE RESISTANCE OF TIMBER*

Robert H. Leicester**

Introduction

The combustibility of timber and the potential of timber to fuel a fire have been a stumbling block to the rational development of procedures for assessing the fire safety of timber structures. The basis for this probably lies in history, when cities of timber buildings were devastated by major fires. Well-known examples of this are the fire of London in 1666 and the burning of the Ginza district in Tokyo in 1872. In London, one response was to double the premium for houses having timber frames; in Tokyo, the governor ordered the area to be rebuilt in brick.

A legacy of these past disasters is that in most countries today, the building regulations provide no rational approach to the use of combustible materials, such as timber, for structural purposes. Usually, the regulations either prohibit or accept, without question, the use of such materials for a given end use.

However, during the past few decades there has been a keen interest among fire-research scientists in developing rational procedures for designing timber structures to resist fire. It is probably for this reason, perhaps even more than for reasons related to economic pressures of the building industry, that the situation has been reviewed by building authorities.

This chapter discusses several significant aspects of the behaviour of timber structures in a fire.

A. Characteristics of timber subjected to fire

Wood comprises a mixture of cellulose, hemicellulose and lignin, bound together in a complex network. As wood is heated above 280° C, it decomposes or pyrolyses and is converted to gases, tar and charcoal [1]. The gases flame vigorously at temperatures above 280° C, but the charcoal requires temperatures of about 500° C for it to be consumed.

As the char builds up, it tends to protect the unburnt timber from rapid pyrolysis. The unburnt timber is an excellent thermal insulator and, as a result, the timber a short distance from the char edge is unaffected by the fire. One significant consequence of this is that a timber member in a fire does not exhibit the destructive expansion behaviour of unprotected steel members.

A schematic illustration of burning wood is shown in figure 8. For a softwood, typical parameters of the unburnt timber are as follows [2]: density = 500 kg/m^3; thermal conductivity = 0.15 J/sec m °C; specific heat = 1,700 J/kg °C.

---

*Owing to recent developments in timber engineering and design with respect to fire resistance, the original lecture material has been replaced by this article, which was originally published by the Institution of Engineers (Australia) as chapter 9 of Fire Engineering for Building Structures and Safety.

**An officer of CSIRO, Division of Building Research, Melbourne.

Figure 8. Degradation zones during burning of timber

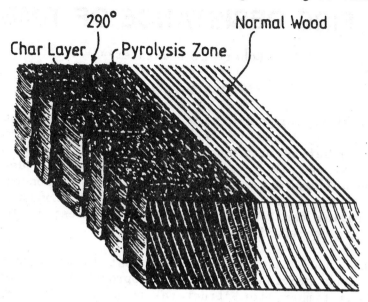

The effect of temperature on strength and stiffness, both during and after a fire, is shown in figures 9 and 10.

Figure 9. Effect of elevated temperatures on the strength and stiffness of wood

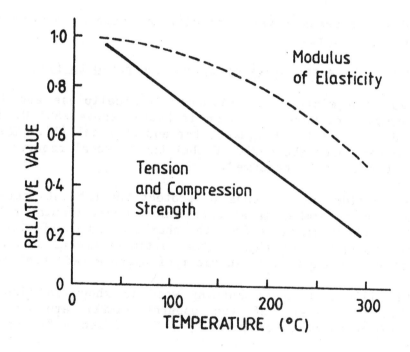

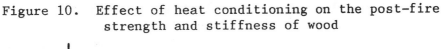

Figure 10.   Effect of heat conditioning on the post-fire
strength and stiffness of wood

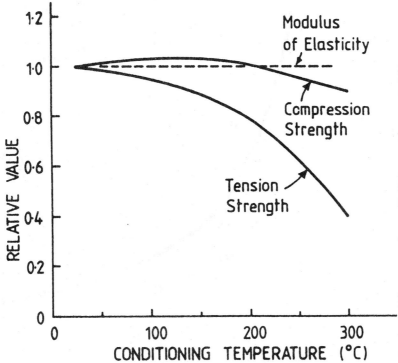

When dry wood is first heated it will char at a rate proportional to the incident radiation [3]:

$$dh/dt = 10 \ R/\rho \qquad (1)$$

where dh/dt is the rate of char (mm/min), R is the radiation (kw/m²) and ρ is the wood density (kg/m³).

Once the wood has developed a protective layer of char, the char rate will slow down considerably. In a standard furnace test, as specified in AS 1530.4-1985 [4], dry wood will char for several hours at a roughly constant rate [5]:

$$dh/dt = 0.5 + (250/\rho)^2 \qquad (2)$$

For a typical softwood of density 500 kg/m³, this gives a charring rate of 0.75 mm/min.

The charring rate in a furnace for a range of Australian species is given in figure 11. Values for charring rates from various countries have been collated by Schaffer [6].

1.   Combustibility

The assessment of combustibility given in AS 1530.1-1984 [7] is measured by placing small 45-mm diameter specimens in a calorimeter and heating them to about 800° C for 30 min. If flaming or a temperature rise in the calorimeter is noted, then combustion is deemed to have occurred. According to this criterion, timber, even timber treated with fire retardants, is classified as combustible.

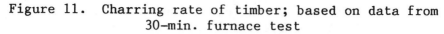

Figure 11. Charring rate of timber; based on data from
30-min. furnace test

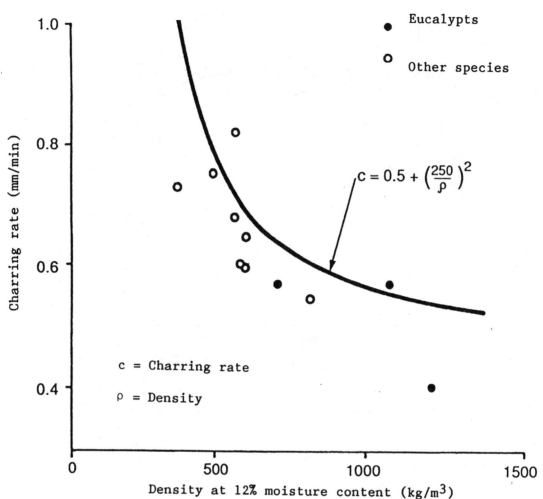

If the purpose of the combustibility test is to reduce the fuel load in building fires, then this does not appear to be a rational basis for banning the use of timber as a structural material. For a start, it is quite an easy matter to design a timber structure that contributes less than 20 per cent of the fuel loading of a building. In addition, timber is not the most dangerous of the fuels that are to be found in buildings. This is indicated by the comparison of the burning rates of some selected materials as shown in table 6.

Of more concern than combustibility is the phenomenon of after-glow, which is the ability of exothermic materials such as timber to continue burning after the external heat source has been removed. This can occur in timber treated with CCA wood preservative after only a few seconds of contact with a grass fire; in this case the risk of after-glow can be minimized by replacing CCA with the CSIRO-patented 3S formulation, which is based on zinc and phosphorus additives. After-glow can also occur in untreated timber if it is subjected to a fierce fire for more than 30 minutes; treatment with a suitable fire retardant will remove the risk of this happening. In urban fires, the risk of after-glow is negligible, as firemen have been trained to douse burnt timber with water.

Table 6.   Ideal burning rates a/

Material	Ideal burning rate $(g/cm^2\ sec \times 10^4)$
Ethyl alcohol	40
Polystyrene	35
Polycarbonate	25
Douglas fir	13

Source: A. Tewarson and R. F. Pion, "Flammability of plastics - I. Burning intensity", Combustion and Flame, No. 26, 1976, pp. 85-103.

a/ The ideal burning rate is defined as the combustion rate when energy losses from the burning surface equal the energy supplied by other bodies.

2. Early fire hazard

The initial stages of a fire, before flash-over occurs, are usually the most dangerous with respect to human safety. This risk may be assessed by AS 1530.3-1982 [8]. Some hazard values measured in this way are shown in tables 7, 8 and 9. The range of the hazard index is 0-20 for ignition and 0-10 for the other parameters. Zero indicates a negligible hazard.

Table 7. Hazard indices for some building materials

Material	Hazard index			
	Ignition	Flame spread	Heat evolved	Smoke developed
Plasterboard	12	0	2	3
Pine	15	7	6	3
Acrylic carpet	16	8	9	6

Source: J. Beesley, J. J. Keough and A. W. Moulen, "Early burning properties of Australian timbers", Technical Paper (Second Series) No. 6 (Melbourne, CSIRO, Division of Building Research, 1974).

Table 8. Hazard indices for untreated timber

Timber density (kg/m^3)	Hazard index			
	Ignition	Flame spread	Heat evolved	Smoke developed
400	14	9	9	4
900	13	5	5	2

Source: A. W. Moulen and S. J. Grubits, "The early fire hazard properties of timbers", Technical Study No. 50 (Canberra, Experimental Building Station, Department of Housing and Construction, Australian Government Publishing Services, 1980).

Table 9. Hazard indices for radiata pine

Treatment	Hazard index			
	Ignition	Flame spread	Heat evolved	Smoke developed
Untreated	15	7	6	3
Impregnated with fire retardant	0	0	0	2

Source: J. Beesley, J. J. Keough and A. W. Moulen, "Early burning properties of Australian timbers", Technical Paper (Second Series) No. 6 (Melbourne, CSIRO, Division of Building Research, 1974).

Tables 7 and 9 show that the hazard of an untreated softwood timber is no worse than that of acceptable furnishings, such as acrylic carpet, but certainly nowhere near as good as that of plasterboard. Table 8 shows that the hazard indices tend to drop with increasing density of the timber; table 9 shows that the early fire hazard of timber can be essentially eliminated by the use of fire retardant treatments.

Gardner and Thomson [9] have conducted full-scale room burn tests and obtained the time to flash-over for a variety of forest products. Some of these are listed in table 10, and it can be seen that there is reasonable correlation between time to flash-over and the AS 1530.3 time to ignition and the ASTM E84 flame spread index [10]. There was very poor correlation between the time to flash-over and either the spread of flame or heat-evolved indices evaluated according to AS 1530.3. It should be noted that the AS 1530.3 spread of flame index is currently used as the method of regulating building materials in Australia.

Table 10. Measured early fire hazard properties of forest products

Material	Density (kg/m^3)	Time to flash-over in room burn (min)	AS 1530.3 time to ignition (min)	ASTM E84 flame spread index
Fire-retardant-treated				
Sawn radiata pine	532	No flash-over	15.4	6
Untreated				
Sawn blackbutt	952	7.2	6.5	48
Sawn Douglas fir	498	6.5	5.5	69
Sawn Victorian ash	654	6.3	6.2	51
Sawn radiata pine	532	6.1	5.7	77
Sawn Western red cedar	345	5.9	5.0	69
Radiata pine particle board	754	5.6	5.1	104
Luan plywood	480	4.5	4.6	170

3. Structural integrity

Once flash-over occurs and the contents of a compartment become fully involved in a fire, it is necessary to prevent this fire from spreading to adjacent compartments. The defence mechanism against this requires not only that the integrity of the compartment walls remain intact but also that the supporting structure maintain its load-carrying function during the fire.

The assessment of structural performance in a fire may be carried out according to AS 1530.4-1985, which specifies that a structural element, or system, be loaded to its intended design load and then subjected to a furnace fire that is intended to simulate the conditions of a fiercely raging compartment fire. The time to collapse of the structural element, or system, is deemed to be the fire resistance rating of that element. Most of the proposed fire-resistance design methods for timber structures are related to meeting this furnace-test criterion.

Fire resistance of solid timber elements

For theoretical design procedures, the first step in evaluating the strength of solid timber elements during a fire is to compute the area of unburnt timber and the rate at which the char is progressing. For a furnace test, this can be done through the use of equation (2).

Then, the wood temperature at a distance x in from the edge of the char can be evaluated from

$$T = T_0 + (T_{max} - T_0) \exp (-\alpha x) \tag{3}$$

where

$$\alpha = dh/dt \ \rho C_p/k \tag{4}$$

Here, T_O is 23° C, the initial temperature of the wood; T_{max} is 290° C, the temperature at the edge of the char; dh/dt is the charring rate; ρ is the density; Cp is the specific heat; and k is the thermal conductivity.

Figure 12 shows the temperature distribution computed in this way for a softwood timber subjected to a standard furnace test. From this information and that given in figures 9 and 10, the strength distribution in timber both during and after a fire can be determined, and these are shown in figures 13 and 14.

Figure 12. Temperature distribution in a softwood timber during a fire

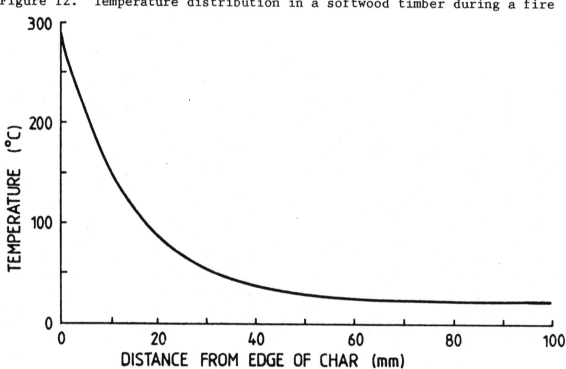

Figure 13. Structural properties of solid timber during a fire

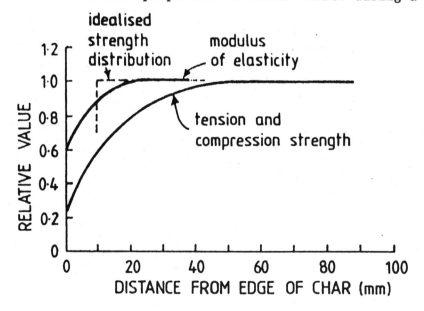

Figure 14.   Structural properties of solid timber after a fire

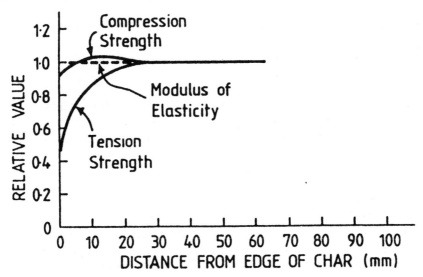

It is seen that during a fire, a realistic assessment of structural behaviour can be obtained by neglecting a 10-mm layer of unburnt timber and assuming that the residue still has its full initial strength and stiffness. Similar results have been obtained recently by Schaffer and others [11].

Fire resistance of metal connectors

Unprotected metal connector systems exhibit very poor performance in fires. The connectors conduct the external temperatures rapidly, and when the wood reaches 300° C it loses all its local bearing strength, as indicated in figure 9. When this happens, the connector system fails [12].

The simplest method of protecting metal connectors is by recessing them into the timber of the structural member and then covering them with an additional glued-in plug of timber (figure 15).

Figure 15.   A method of protecting metal connectors

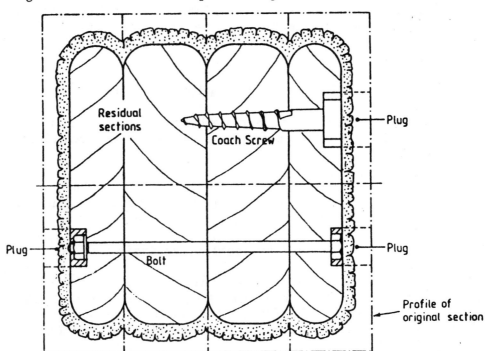

Glued joints

Fire does not burn any faster in glued joints than it does in solid timber. However, the strength of glued joints may fall rapidly as the temperature rises. For example, urea formaldehyde glue tends to lose significant strength at 100° C.

The presence of glued joints may be ignored when these are only lightly stressed and occur in bulky members such as glulam. However, in small, highly stressed situations such as occur with finger-jointed scantling, the glued joint should not be relied on to perform well unless it is first checked by a fire performance test.

Repair of fire-damaged structures

After a mild fire, heavy timber members may be quite satisfactory for continued service. As indicated in figure 14, there is an effective loss of strength to a depth of about 5.0 mm below the charred depth. Frequently this is of no consequence for members whose sizes have been determined by stiffness considerations, and in such cases the unsightly char is usually sandblasted off and the surface repainted. Metal connectors should be checked to ensure that they are intact and that they have the necessary protection to make them fire resistant.

B.   Recent developments

1.   Performance in furnace tests

The performance in a standard furnace test, such as that described in AS 1530, is used as a basis for fire resistance ratings.

There have been many measurements of the effects of a furnace test on the load capacity of solid timber and glulam beams [13], [14], [15]. For standard metal connectors, the fire resistance is poor, usually less than 15 min [12]. For modified connector systems, German standard DIN 4102.4 [16] and Meyer-Ottens [17] provide fire resistance figures based on furnace tests.

Data on the performance characteristics of various wall and floor assemblies containing timber elements may be obtained from such organizations as the Underwriter's Laboratories of Canada [18] and from building regulatory authories [16], [19], [20], [21].

2.   Room fires and building tests

The charring rates of timber members in room fires have been studied extensively, and effective prediction methods are available for softwood timbers [19], [22].

Full-scale tests on small two-storey buildings have been undertaken in Japan [23], which show that light-frame timber construction can provide satisfactory fire resistance for dwellings.

3.   Reliability analysis

Reliability methods of analysis for assessing the fire resistance of timber structures have been developed both for the case of furnace fires with a steady charring rate [24], [25], [26] and for the case of room fires [19], [27]. Mehaffey [28] used reliability and physical modelling concepts to assess the effects of the added fire severity due to the use of wood studs in fire separation walls and found that the added effects were neglible.

4. Standards

Existing standards and draft standards on the fire resistance of timber construction are all based in some way on the furnace test. Some standards give the fire resistance directly in terms of furnace test data [16], [21], [29]. Others standards are formatted in terms of computing the residual strength after subtracting a sacrificial layer of char [30], [31]. In the Australian draft standard, the residual strength is taken to be equal to the strength at ambient temperatures.

The first edition of the Building Code of Australia accepts the use of fire-resistance-rated timber elements for certain classes of buildings. However, for other classes there is a restriction on the use of timber because it is classed as a combustible material. This restriction holds regardless of how well the structure performs under fire conditions and regardless of how little it may contribute to the fire hazard. The reasons for such a restriction have not been stated clearly.

References

1. E. L. Schaffer, "Effect of pyrolytic temperatures on the longitudinal strength of dry Douglas-fir", Journal of Testing and Evaluation, vol. 1, No. 4 (July 1973), pp. 319-329.

2. R. M. Knudsen and A. P. Schniewind, "Performance of structural wood members exposed to fire", Forest Products Journal, vol. 25, No. 2 (February 1975), pp. 23-32.

3. E. G. Butcher, "The yule log - do we know how fast it burns?", Fire Surveyor, December 1976, pp. 29-33.

4. Standards Association of Australia, Australian Standard 1530.4: Methods for Fire Tests on Building Materials, Components and Structures: Part 4 - Fire-resistance Tests of Elements of Building Construction (Sydney, 1985).

5. R. H. Leicester, "Challenges to research on wood engineering - south-east Asian/Australasian point of view", Proceedings of 1988 International Conference on Timber Engineering (Seattle, Washington, September 1988).

6. E. L. Schaffer, "Structural fire design: wood", Research paper FPL 450 (Madison, Wisconsin, USA, United States Department of Agriculture, Forest Products Research Laboratory, October 1984).

7. Standards Association of Australia, Australian Standard 1530.1: Methods for Fire Tests on Building Materials, Components and Structures: Part 1 - Combustibility Test for Materials (Sydney, 1984).

8. Standards Association of Australia, Australian Standard 1530.3: Methods for Fire Tests on Building Materials and Structures: Test for Early Fire Hazard Properties of Materials (Sydney, 1982).

9. W. D. Gardner and C. R. Thomson, "Flame spread properties of forest products - comparison and validation of Australian and North American flame spread test methods", Technical Paper No. 36 (Sydney, Forestry Commission of New South Wales, 1987).

10. American Society for Testing and Materials, <u>Standard Test Method for Sur-face Burning Characteristics of Building Materials</u> (Philadelphia, 1988), E 84.

11. E. L. Schaffer and others, "Strength validation and fire endurance of glued-laminated timber beams", Research Paper FPL 467 (Madison, Wisconsin, USA, United States Department of Agriculture, Forest Products Research Laboratory, February 1986).

12. R. H. Leicester, C. A. Seath and L. Pham, "The fire resistance of metal connectors", <u>Proceedings of 19th Forests Products Research Conference</u> (Melbourne, CSIRO, Division of Chemical and Wood Technology, 1979).

13. T. T. Lie, "A method for assessing the fire resistance of laminated tim-ber beams and columns", DBR Paper No. 718 (Ottawa, Canada, National Research Council of Canada, Division of Building Research, June 1977).

14. K. Imaizumi, "Stability in fire of protected and unprotected glued lamin-ated beams", <u>Norsk Skogind</u>, vol. 16, No. 4 (1963), pp. 140-151.

15. H. Dorn and K. Egner, "Fire tests on glued laminated structural timbers (glulam beams)", National Research Council of Canada Technical Transla-tion 1131, translation by D. A. Sinclair (Ottawa, Canada, National Research Council, Division of Building Research, 1964).

16. Deutsches Institut für Normung e. V., <u>DIN 4102: Part 4 - Fire Behaviour of Building Materials and Building Components</u> (Berlin, Germany, Beuth Verlag, March 1981).

17. C. Meyer-Ottens, "Junctions in wood structures - total construction", <u>Proceedings of International Seminar on Three Decades of Structural Fire Safety</u> (Boreham Wood, Hertfordshire, UK, Fire Research Station, Building Research Establishment, Department of Environment, February 1983), pp. 247-259.

18. Underwriter's Laboratories of Canada, <u>List of Equipment and Materials: Building Construction</u> (Scarborough, Ontario, Canada, September 1986), vol. II.

19. R. Jönsson and O. Pettersson, <u>Timber Structures and Fire: A Review of the Existing State of Knowledge and Research Requirements</u> (Stockholm, Sweden, Swedish Council for Building Research, 1985).

20. Standards Association of New Zealand, <u>Miscellaneous Publication 9/7: Fire Resistance Ratings of Floor/Ceiling Combinations</u> (Wellington, 1966).

21. National Research Council of Canada, <u>Supplement to the National Building Code: NRCC No. 23178</u> (Ottawa, 1985), pp. 42-44, 55-56.

22. S. Hadvig, <u>Charring of Wood in Building Fires: Practice, Theory, Instru-mentation, Measurements</u> (Lyngby, Denmark, Technical University of Denmark, Laboratory of Heating and Air-Conditioning, 1981).

23. Koichi Kishitani, Shinichi Sugahara and Hiroshi Sato, "Behaviour in fire of timber-frame residential buildings as tested by single-room models", <u>Journal of the Faculty of Engineering</u>, vol. 36, No. 3 (Tokyo, 1982), pp. 529-548.

24. F. E. Woeste and E. L. Schaffer, "Second moment reliability analysis of fire-exposed wood floor joist assemblies", <u>Fire and Materials</u>, vol. 3, No. 3 (1979), pp. 126-131.

25. F. E. Woeste and E. L. Schaffer, "Reliability analysis of fire-exposed light-frame wood floor assemblies", Research Paper FPL 386 (Madison, Wisconsin, USA, United States Department of Agriculture, Forest Products Research Laboratory, January 1981).

26. D. A. Bender and others, "Reliability formulation for the strength and fire endurance of glued-laminated beams", Research Paper FPL 460 (Madison, Wisconsin, USA, United States Department of Agriculture, Forest Products Research Laboratory, 1985).

27. O. Pettersson and R. Jönsson, "Reliability based design of fire-exposed timber structures – state of art and summary design guide", Report LUTVDG/TVBB-3040 (Lund, Sweden, Lund University, Institute of Science and Technology, Department of Fire Safety Engineering, 1988).

28. J. Mehaffey, "The contribution of wood-studs to fire severity", Report prepared for Canadian Wood Council (Fredericton, New Brunswick, Canada, December 1987).

29. Council of American Building Officials, "Design of one-hour fire-resistive exposed wood members (6-inch nominal or greater)", Report No. NER-250 (Birmingham, Alabama, USA, 1985).

30. Standards Association of Australia, <u>Draft 83201: Timber Engineering Code: Part 4 – Fire Resistance of Timber Structures</u> (Sydney, 1983).

31. British Standards Institution, <u>British Standard 5268 – Code of Practice for the Structural Use of Timber: Part 4 – Fire Resistance of Timber Structures: Section 4.1 – Method of Calculating Fire Resistance of Timber Members</u> (London, 1978).

UNIDO GENERAL STUDIES SERIES

The following publications are available in this series:

Title	Symbol	Price (US$)
Planning and Programming the Introduction of CAD/CAM Systems 　A reference guide for developing countries	ID/SER.O/1	25.00
Value Analysis in the Furniture Industry	ID/SER.O/2	7.00
Production Management for Small- and Medium-Scale Furniture Manufacturers 　A manual for developing countries	ID/SER.O/3	10.00
Documentation and Information Systems for Furniture and Joinery Plants 　A manual for developing countries	ID/SER.O/4	20.00
Low-cost Prefabricated Wooden Houses 　A manual for developing countries	ID/SER.O/5	6.00
Timber Construction for Developing Countries 　Introduction to wood and timber engineering	ID/SER.O/6	20.00
Timber Construction for Developing Countries 　Structural timber and related products	ID/SER.O/7	25.00
Timber Construction for Developing Countries 　Durability and fire resistance	ID/SER.O/8	20.00
Timber Construction for Developing Countries 　Strength characteristics and design	ID/SER.O/9	25.00
Timber Construction for Developing Countries 　Applications and examples	ID/SER.O/10	20.00
Technical Criteria for the Selection of Woodworking Machines	ID/SER.O/11	25.00
Issues in the Commercialization of Biotechnology	ID/SER.O/13	45.00
Software Industry 　Current trends and implications for developing countries	ID/SER.O/14	25.00
Maintenance Management Manual 　With special reference to developing countries	ID/SER.O/15	35.00
Manual for Small Industrial Businesses 　Project design and appraisal	ID/SER.O/16	25.00

Forthcoming titles include:

Design and Manufacture of Bamboo and Rattan Furniture	ID/SER.O/12	

Please add US$ 2.50 per copy to cover postage and packing. Allow 4-6 weeks for delivery.

ORDER FORM

Please complete this form and return it to:

UNIDO Documents Unit (F-355)
Vienna International Centre
P.O. Box 300, A-1400 Vienna, Austria

Send me _____ copy/copies of _____

_____ (ID/SER.O/_____) at US$ _____ /copy plus postage.

PAYMENT

☐ I enclose a cheque, money order or UNESCO coupon (obtainable from UNESCO offices worldwide) made payable to "UNIDO".

☐ I have made payment through the following UNIDO bank account: CA-BV, No. 29-05115 (ref. RB-7310000), Schottengasse 6, A-1010 Vienna, Austria.

Name _____

Address _____

Telephone _____ Telex _____ Cable _____ Fax _____

Note: Publications in this series may also be obtained from:

Sales Section	Sales Unit
United Nations	United Nations
Room DC2-0853	Palais des Nations
New York, N.Y. 10017, U.S.A.	CH-1211 Geneva 10, Switzerland
Tel.: (212) 963-8302	Tel.: (22) 34-60-11, ext. Bookshop

ORDER FORM

Please complete this form and return it to:

UNIDO Documents Unit (F-355)
Vienna International Centre
P.O. Box 300, A-1400 Vienna, Austria

Send me _____ copy/copies of _____

_____ (ID/SER.O/_____) at US$ _____ /copy plus postage.

PAYMENT

☐ I enclose a cheque, money order or UNESCO coupon (obtainable from UNESCO offices worldwide) made payable to "UNIDO".

☐ I have made payment through the following UNIDO bank account: CA-BV, No. 29-05115 (ref. RB-7310000), Schottengasse 6, A-1010 Vienna, Austria.

Name _____

Address _____

Telephone _____ Telex _____ Cable _____ Fax _____

Note: Publications in this series may also be obtained from:

Sales Section	Sales Unit
United Nations	United Nations
Room DC2-0853	Palais des Nations
New York, N.Y. 10017, U.S.A.	CH-1211 Geneva 10, Switzerland
Tel.: (212) 963-8302	Tel.: (22) 34-60-11, ext. Bookshop